TRACING YOUR ANCESTORS THROUGH COUNTY RECORDS

FAMILY HISTORY FROM PEN & SWORD

TRACING YOUR ANCESTORS THROUGH COUNTY RECORDS

A Guide for Family and Local Historians

Stuart A. Raymond

Pen & Sword
FAMILY HISTORY

First published in Great Britain in 2016
PEN & SWORD FAMILY HISTORY
an imprint of
Pen & Sword Books Ltd
47 Church Street,
Barnsley
South Yorkshire,
S70 2AS

ISBN 978 1 47383 363 0

A CIP catalogue record for this book is
available from the British Library.

Typeset in Palatino and Optima by CHIC GRAPHICS

Printed and bound in England by
CPI Group (UK), Croydon, CR0 4YY

Pen & Sword Books Ltd incorporates the imprints of Pen & Sword
Archaeology, Atlas, Aviation, Battleground, Discovery, Family History,
History, Maritime, Military, Naval, Politics, Railways, Select, Social History,
Transport, True Crime, Claymore Press, Frontline Books, Leo Cooper,
Praetorian Press, Remember When, Seaforth Publishing and Wharncliffe.

For a complete list of Pen & Sword titles please contact
PEN & SWORD BOOKS LTD
47 Church Street, Barnsley, South Yorkshire, S70 2AS, England
E-mail: enquiries@pen-and-sword.co.uk
Website: www.pen-and-sword.co.uk

CONTENTS

A box of Quarter Sessions documents. What might they tell you? (Wiltshire & Swindon History Centre)

INTRODUCTION

The lives of the 'plain English folk' depicted in the records of Quarter Sessions and Assizes, 'are the fountain from which the crowd of Shakespeare's characters is derived. Every one of his squires, constables, serving men, labourers, clowns, drunkards, and other picturesque villains have their real prototypes' in the pages of these records.[1] If history is about people, then anyone aspiring to study the history of ordinary English people needs to consult the Quarter Sessions order books, sessions rolls and other archives preserved in county record offices.

Many people who use these offices do not realise that their original purpose was to preserve the records of Quarter Sessions. Nor do they appreciate the extent of those records, the diverse information that can be found in them and the possibilities for research that they present. The aim of this book is primarily to provide a detailed handbook to English and Welsh Quarter Sessions records, to describe the background to the various different record series and to suggest how they might be used. The duties of Lord Lieutenants, Sheriffs, Assize judges and other county officers were intimately linked with Quarter Sessions, and their records will also be discussed (see Chapters 1, 2, 11 and 12).

England was divided into shires, as the Anglo-Saxons called them, at an early date. The Normans called them counties. For administrative purposes, they were divided up into Hundreds (Wapentakes in the North, Rapes in Sussex, Lathes in Kent), which had their own officers. Hundreds consisted of a number of parishes, which also had their own officers. These were the areas over which Quarter Sessions and related authorities exercised their jurisdictions. In Wales, the shires were not created until 1536.

English Quarter Sessions began in the fourteenth century. Their archives do not generally survive before the sixteenth century, although some fourteenth-century records are in The National Archives. Most of the information in this book relates to the period between the sixteenth and the nineteenth centuries. The administrative functions of Quarter Sessions ended in 1888, when County Councils were created. The records of County Councils and other post-1888 local government institutions will not be dealt with here. Nor will the post-1888 judicial functions of Quarter Sessions, which continued to be exercised for almost another century. The Justice of the Peace, of course, continues to adjudicate today.

Justices of the Peace were also intimately linked with parish officers. The records of parish government have already been described in my *Tracing Your Ancestors' Parish Records: A Guide for Family and Local Historians* (Pen & Sword, 2015), which should be read alongside the present volume.

This book also deals with the records of some other pre-1888 institutions of local government, such as turnpike trusts and commissioners for sewers. However, separate books would be needed to review the records of boroughs, and of Poor Law Unions. Many boroughs had their own Quarter Sessions and Justices of the Peace. Their activities were partially governed by borough charters, and will not be dealt with here.[2] Nor will the various liberties – such as Havering at Bower (Essex), the Isle of Ely (Cambridgeshire) and the Hundred of Launditch (Norfolk) – which were exempt from the jurisdiction of county Quarter Sessions. The activities of Justices and other county officers in collecting national taxation will not be discussed in detail.

Before 1732, many records are in Latin. It is not, however, always good Latin; the scribes of the Restoration order book in Surrey demonstrated their unfamiliarity with the language by making many corrections and re-corrections. Fortunately for them, they were able to write the majority of the text in English. The Latin used in old documents is frequently repetitive; much useful phraseology is translated in Brooke Westcott's *Making Sense of Latin Documents for Family & Local Historians* (Family History Press, 2014). For a useful introduction to Latin, see Denis Stuart's *Latin for Local and Family Historians: A Beginner's Guide* (Phillimore, 1995).

I have drawn heavily on the catalogues of county record offices, and of The National Archives, both printed and online. A great deal of information has been found on the Discovery database http://discovery.nationalarchives.gov.uk. Online catalogues of record offices generally give more up-to-date information than their printed versions, many of which date back decades. Although the latter still give valuable overviews, and much useful general information, recourse has to be made to the internet for detailed information.

A number of sources discussed here have been digitized, transcribed, or abstracted, and are available on the internet, sometimes on pay-to-view sites. Many transcripts and abstracts of particular sources have been published by local record societies and others. These are very useful to researchers; quite apart from the intrinsic interest of the documents themselves, they frequently include detailed introductions which place the documents in their context, and explain how and why they came into being. Record society publications are listed at http://royalhistsoc.org/publications/national-regional-history.

The lists of further reading given in each chapter are not intended as full bibliographies, but merely indications of works that I have found useful. Much more can be found by searching library catalogues and the internet. Note too that many of the older works mentioned here have been digitized, and are available on websites such as www.archive.org and www.hathitrust.org.

My major debt in writing this book is to the many archivists who have catalogued and described their holdings, and to the many editors who have prepared record society volumes. There have been fewer general studies of county government, but I am indebted to those that have been written. They are cited at appropriate points in my text. Drafts of this book were read by Simon Fowler and by one of my Pharos students who wishes to remain anonymous; both made useful comments and saved me from errors. Those that remain are of course my responsibility. Please let me know if you find any.

Chapter 1

LORD LIEUTENANTS AND THE MILITIA

Lord Lieutenants were first appointed by Henry VIII. Commissions placed Sheriffs (see Chapter 2), who held titular command of county forces, under the command of the Lieutenancy. The earliest were issued in June 1545, 'to endure until Michaelmas'. Lord John Russell, as one of the earliest Lieutenants, found himself commanding the Crown's forces against the Prayer Book Rebellion in 1549. Queen Elizabeth only made intermittent appointments, until the threat of Spanish invasion prompted appointments for most counties in 1585.

Henceforward, the office was normally held for life. Frequently, several counties were included in one Commission. Lieutenants' jurisdictions generally included boroughs and liberties otherwise exempt from county authorities. The actual title, Lord Lieutenant, was used for the first time in an Act of 1557–8. Commissions were frequently – but not always – issued by letters patent, under the Great Seal. They can be found on the Patent Rolls (National Archives series C 66). Justices of the Peace were placed under the Lieutenancy; they had to be 'attendante, aydinge, assistinge, counsellinge, helpinge, and at the [Lieutenant's] commandement'.[1] In 1559, even the Assize judges took instructions from the Lord Lieutenant of London.[2]

The *raison d'être* of the Lieutenancy was defence. Most routine duties connected with the Militia were undertaken by deputies (see below). Lord Lieutenants were the principal representatives of the Crown in the counties, and expected to represent the interests of their county to the Crown. Until the Civil War, they were frequently more attentive to localist demands than to those of the Crown. They mediated quarrels between gentlemen in their Lieutenancies; the government was determined that 'they would at all costs not allow quarrelling among

John Russell, Earl of Bedford, one of the first Lord Lieutenants.

those who served them'.[3] It was too dangerous. They directed the campaign against Roman Catholicism (see Chapter 9), and supervised the punishment of vagabonds (see Chapter 8). They administered forced loans, such as those imposed by Elizabeth in 1589[4] and by Charles I in 1626.[5] Militia rates and purveyance were under their supervision.[6] They assisted the government's abortive attempt to introduce a native silk industry.[7] The Deputy Lieutenants of Northamptonshire were even asked to sell lottery tickets to raise money for the plantation of Virginia![8] In the 1680s, Lieutenants played a leading role in purging borough corporations of radical elements.

The position of Lord Lieutenant was a senior appointment, usually held by a member of the Privy Council or the nobility. Under Elizabeth, Lord Burghley himself served for Hertfordshire. The appointment of peers to the office was royal acknowledgement of their dominance in society, giving them greater status, power and patronage. They influenced the appointment of Justices of the Peace, and the election of Members of Parliament.

Their position, however, depended heavily on the Crown's favour. When the interests of Crown and county clashed, as they began to do in the 1630s, Lord Lieutenants had an unresolvable problem. The impossibility of meeting the expectations of both Crown and county during the 1639 Bishops' War against Scotland reduced the Lieutenancy to total ineffectuality. Control of the Militia was the critical issue in 1642, as the country divided into Royalists and Parliamentarians. Under the Militia Ordinance, Parliament appointed its own Lord Lieutenants,[9] who promptly raised an army. Between 1655 and 1657 Lieutenants were replaced by the Major Generals, chosen for their loyalty to the regime, and funded by the hated decimation tax on Royalists.

After the Restoration, the gentry recognised that strong government was their best defence against the return of the Commonwealth. The Lieutenancy received more support, and was able to put the interests of the Crown before local interests. Charles II chose his Lieutenants primarily for their loyalty, rather than their social standing (although that remained important), and deputies became more diligent. The Militia Acts of 1661 and 1662 gave Lieutenants Parliamentary authority to levy horse and foot, with arms and ammunition, from property owners.[10] They had summary jurisdiction over military matters, and could direct Justices of the Peace. Militia defaulters were regularly summoned before Deputy Lieutenants and fined, rather than reported to the Privy Council. Many fines are recorded in Lieutenancy order books.

Restoration Lieutenants became the channel through which Crown patronage was distributed, replacing the Assize judges (see Chapter 12). They nominated men for appointment to office, and supported their clients wishing to purchase Crown lands. They were, however, unwilling to relax anti-Catholic measures. Their reluctance to sound out the gentry on Catholic emancipation led James II to purge his Lieutenancy – and fatally weaken it.[11] His attempt to replace Royalist Anglicans with Roman Catholics proved disastrous: the gentry felt sidelined, the government was weakened, and the King lost his crown.

Lord Lieutenants gradually became remote figureheads. Their control was frequently both distant and intermittent, given their other duties in government. Their routine work was normally undertaken by Deputy Lieutenants, and by other Justices of the Peace. Deputies were first appointed in 1569. Lieutenants generally chose their deputies personally, subject to the Crown's approval. Warrants for appointments are in The National Archives, series SP 44. Appointments were gazetted in the *London Gazette* from 1665.[12] Deputy Lieutenants only served for one county. They were leading gentry, usually Justices of the Peace. Many were Members of Parliament. By c.1600, there were usually four or five in each county. Numbers tripled or quadrupled under the later Stuarts, as political patronage became an increasingly important element in their appointment. The work was frequently coordinated by a single Deputy, such as Lord Poulett in pre-Civil War Somerset. The position was prestigious, but onerous. One complained that 'if aught were well done the Lieutenant has the praise and thanks though all the charge and travail is borne by us, but if any business has ill success, the blame is laid upon us'.[13] Their basic tasks were to recruit and train the Militia, and to keep tabs on disaffection – a particularly important task after the Restoration, when there was thought to be a serious threat from the 'Good Old Cause'.

Everyone was liable for military service, and expected to provide their own weapons.[14] Men were required (at least until c.1600) to regularly practise archery at the butts erected in every parish. Noblemen, bishops, the gentry, and wealthy yeomen, were expected to maintain their own private armouries. Increasingly, public county, borough and parish armouries were provided, necessitated by the soaring cost of providing ammunition for practice. Centralised armouries equipped the Trained Bands, and were drawn on by men being sent overseas.

Deputies conducted musters, ensured that beacons were maintained, assessed their fellow gentry's liability to supply arms and horse, imposed Militia rates, and paid coat and conduct money to troops raised for overseas service for their clothing and travel. They appointed officers of horse and foot, and clerks to keep records. In Derbyshire, a clerk was paid £13 13s 4d for 'attendinge the musters, writing manie warrants, inrolinge & certifieinge all the forces, & altering & keeping theire muster bookes'.[15] Clerks wrote warrants to summon musters, collect the lists of able men that constables compiled, prepared certificates for the Lord Lieutenant and the Privy Council, and copied them into the Lieutenancies' own muster books. Routine administration took up a considerable amount of time, to the detriment of any personal involvement by the Deputies in training.

There were two types of musters. General musters, sometimes with several points of assembly, were regularly held. Attendance was compulsory. Horse and foot might be mustered separately. 'All hable persons' aged between sixteen and sixty were summoned to appear. Arms and men had to be 'shown': the word 'muster' derives from the Latin *monstrare* – to show. High constables took men's names, and assessed their wealth to determine their liability to bear arms. Many papers relating to their assessments can be found in Lieutenancy letter books. After 1662, those with an income of £500 per annum, or an estate valued at £6,000, had to provide a horse. An armed foot soldier was required from those who had £50 per annum, or an estate valued at over £600.

A 'reasonable number' of those who attended musters were chosen to be trained, armed and taught how to handle weapons and horses. Others, able to serve as labourers or pioneers, carpenters or smiths, were listed. Those who appeared were paid by a rate on their parish; allowances were paid to the wives of pressed men.

Securing attendance could be difficult. Men were frequently unwilling to appear, and the tardiness and prevarication of unwilling parish constables, responsible for ensuing they did so, could render musters almost pointless. However, defaulters could be compelled to enter a recognizance[16] to do so, and were sometimes indicted at Quarter Sessions.

Special musters were training sessions for small units, sometimes held monthly, weekly, or even daily. In 1573, the government ordered 'a convenient and sufficient number of the most able to be chosen and collected' for training; these formed the Trained Bands. The training was in the new art of gunnery. Bandsmen were recruited from the more prosperous householders and yeoman farmers; in Wiltshire, it was ordered in 1617 that only those who had £2 in land for life, or £40 in goods, should serve.[17]

The Trained Bands provided more effective training than general musters. In 1639, when the Privy Council sent inspectors to report on the Lancashire Militia, Captain Threlwall reported that the footsoldiers of the Trained Bands were 'reasonably well exercised . . . and all able bodied men', and that defects in their armour and weapons were slight. However, he also reported that the horse were neither very able, nor well armed.[18] The latter had probably

A Trained Band Soldier, From Charles Knight. Old England a Pictorial Museum. 1845.

only attended general musters. The horse were generally the most unsatisfactory part of the Militia, as gentlemen could easily evade service.

Special musters have left little trace in the records. Training was left to professional muster masters, who were frequently outsiders, doubly disliked because the gentlemen they trained objected to taking orders from men of less exalted social rank. Their work inevitably suffered from political interference, and from disputes over fees. Elizabethan parsimony required counties to pay them, rather than the Exchequer. Justices frequently refused payment, regarding it as unconstitutional.

Non-commissioned officers frequently had considerable experience of Continental campaigns. Many were maimed soldiers, sometimes given pensions conditional on appearing at musters (see Chapter 7). Deputy Lieutenants were very solicitous of the rights of maimed soldiers; their letters are frequently found amongst Quarter Sessions records endorsing requests for pensions.

After 1589, Lord Lieutenants also appointed Provost Marshalls. They exercised a disciplinary role, apprehending and punishing defaulting soldiers, and dealing with vagrants and other 'masterless men'.[19]

Sometimes, troops had to be raised for actual fighting. In Cambridgeshire, the work of raising 500 foot soldiers and fifty horse for service against a threatened Spanish invasion in 1599 can be traced in the letters of the Lieutenancy. The proceedings of the Devon Lieutenancy when it was ordered to provide 2,000 men to march against Scotland in 1639 can be traced amongst SP series in The National Archives.[20] Indentures listing troops raised for overseas service are in series E101.

During the Interregnum, the Militia was reduced to cavalry reserves for the army, under Cromwell's Major Generals. After the Restoration, the old distinction between the Trained Bands and the rest of the Militia ceased. Personal service from wealthier individuals ceased to be required; they could instead pay £10 per annum. The Militia became primarily an agency for promoting Royalism and repressing survivors of the 'Good Old Cause'. Loyalty was required above all else. The Militia Act of 1662 directed the removal of all those who refused the oaths of allegiance and supremacy. Servants sent in the place of their masters had to be 'well affected'. These precautions were partially successful. When the Duke of Monmouth landed at Lyme Regis (Dorset) in 1685, the Militia succeeded in blocking his route, even though many men deserted to his cause rather than actually fighting him. The officers remained loyal.

Many Tudor and Stuart muster rolls have survived. Some pre-date the establishment of Lord Lieutenancies. The earliest to be noticed here were compiled in 1522, when Cardinal Wolsey used the pretext of a muster to make an in-depth valuation of property, and to assess a forced loan. The 1522 rolls made the customary returns of able-bodied men, arms and harness (body armour), but also made some additions. All men over the age of sixteen 'and whom they belong to' were listed. Occupations were sometimes given. Clergy and aliens were included. So were landowners, with, crucially for Wolsey, the value of their lands. The 1522 rolls enabled the Crown to identify defaulters, who could be compelled to purchase the correct armour; they also identified those able to make 'loans'.[21] Defence required not just men and arms, but also money.

Muster rolls sent to the Privy Council sometimes list all able-bodied men in a parish. Where they record trades, they may enable us to determine the occupational structure of particular communities. The rolls for 1539, 1542 and 1569 are particularly notable, although they continued to be compiled right up until the Civil War. Occasionally, there were separate rolls for clergy. Sixteenth- and seventeenth-century muster rolls may be found in The National Archives, amongst the State Papers, and in series E 36 and E 101.[22] Many Civil War muster rolls and related documents can be found in series SP 28. SP 16 has muster rolls from the Bishops' War in 1639. Other rolls are in local record offices. In some instances, these may have been used to compile those sent to the Privy Council. A few published rolls with useful introductions are listed below.

Apart from the muster rolls, no provision was made for the preservation of early Lieutenancy records; few survive for the Tudor period, although in some counties copies of important papers were made for deputy lieutenants. Better provision was made by the post-Restoration Norfolk Deputy Lieutenants, who ordered a clerk to attend them and 'to enter all such our transactions into our common journal booke'.[23] Many Lieutenancy orders, letter books and journals have been preserved with Quarter Sessions records, and amongst private papers held in institutions such as the British Library, the Bodleian Library and local record offices. Others have been preserved in the Privy Council registers (series PC 2),[24] and amongst the State Papers (SP), in The National Archives. There are printed calendars for many of these series. Some relevant record society publications with useful introductions are listed below. These records provide much information, not only on the Militia, but on subjects as diverse as recusancy, vagrancy, purveyance and economic history.

The early eighteenth-century Militia was largely moribund, except during times of emergency such as the rebellions of 1715 and 1745. However, the threat of Continental war led to the Militia Act of 1757. Militia regiments were to be recruited by conscription, unless sufficient volunteers came forward. Liability to provide men was placed on the parish, rather than on owners of property as previously. Each county had to provide a specific number of men: Middlesex and Devon were both required to raise 1,200, but Rutland a mere 120.[25] Parish constables held ballots to select men liable to serve, unless sufficient volunteers came forward. Substitutes could be sent if those chosen did not wish to serve. Service was for three years; men underwent training for twenty-eight days every year. Militiamen were not liable for service overseas, although some regiments were embodied for prolonged service when war with France broke out in 1778, and again in 1793.

Between 1757 and 1831, the constables' Militia ballot lists listed all adult able-bodied men. Age limits were eighteen to fifty between 1758 and 1762, eighteen to forty-five between 1762 and 1831. There were certain exemptions, varying over time: men such as clergy, apprentices, magistrates, constables, serving soldiers, men under 5 feet 4 inches tall, the infirm, and fathers with a large family to support. The information given on the lists also varied. Originally, only names and infirmities were given. After 1758, occupations were required, and after 1802 descriptions and the number of children had to be entered. Other information, such as ages, may also be included. Before ballots took place, lists were displayed on church doors, so that objections to the inclusion or exclusion of particular names could be made. Those conscripted took the oath of allegiance, and their names were entered on a Militia roll. They were then organised into regiments, battalions and companies.

Substantial numbers of Militia ballot lists survive in local record offices. Researchers can frequently rely on them as full censuses of able-bodied adult males. The 1777 list for Northamptonshire has been described as 'the nearest approach to an occupational census' available for the county.[26] However, the exempt, such as clergy and apprentices, who should have been listed, were frequently omitted. They were used to compile a variety of other lists. From 1802, Schedule A lists included both the names of householders aged over forty-five, and women. From these, Schedule B lists were compiled, omitting the two latter categories. After magistrates had heard any appeals against inclusion on these lists, yet more lists were compiled, omitting those exempt from serving. These formed the basis of 'Militia liable books'. Ballots were held not just for the regular Militia, but also for various supplementary forces, such as the 1803–4 Army of Reserve. Separate lists survive for these ballots.

Conscription by ballot was universally hated, and met much opposition. It was suspended in 1829. Militia ballot lists were subsequently compiled in an attempt to reintroduce balloting. However, the ballot was cancelled before it could be held. Henceforward, the Militia consisted of volunteers only.

Militia ballot lists should not be confused with the *Posse Comitatus* lists of 1798, and the *Levée en Masse* lists of 1803–4. These were not compiled for recruitment to the Militia. Rather, the *Posse Comitatus* lists recorded the names, parishes and occupations of all able-bodied men who were not serving, but could be called upon in case of invasion. They were to assist with the evacuation of the civilian population, to remove cattle and crops from the path of the invader, to transport and supply food to troops, and to harry the enemy where possible. These lists provide the researcher with fairly full occupational censuses. Beckett's edition of the *Buckinghamshire Posse Comitatus*[27] has a full listing of the small number of surviving returns nation-wide, and includes a useful critique of the returns.

Levée en Masse lists provided comprehensive listings of men aged from seventeen to fifty-five, with names, occupations and infirmities, arranged in categories according to age, marital status, and number of children aged under ten. Exact ages were sometimes given. The lists included all householders, with their occupations, ages and the numbers of males and females in each household; it identifies Quakers and aliens. Non-combatants needing to be evacuated, including women, children, the old and the infirm, were also listed. Their names, and sometimes their occupations and ages, were noted. Lists of those able to serve as pioneers and special constables were compiled; there were also separate listings of various categories such as millers and waggoners, together with schedules listing cattle, corn and fodder. Few of these lists survive.

Men enlisted served for three years until 1786, five years thereafter. In peacetime, they lived at home, except whilst training. In wartime, they could be stationed anywhere, and usually served outside of their home county. Men are listed on regimental muster and pay lists (National Archives, series WO 13), and on enrolment lists (WO 68 – these include casualty lists). Militia musters 1781–2 (WO 13) have been indexed on CD; for details, visit Family History Indexes – www.fhindexes.co.uk/Militia.htm.

More records survive relating to forces raised during the Napoleonic Wars. The Lieutenancy became involved in the raising of a multitude of voluntary local auxiliary forces, such as Fencibles and Yeomanry. These could be raised and disbanded at will; men joined and left as they wished. Most volunteers were paid only whilst they were in training. The regimental archives of both Volunteers, and of the regular Militia, may now be held in regimental museums or county record offices. Many records are held by The National Archives. Muster rolls and pay lists, 1778 to 1887 are in series WO 13. Related material, such as enrolment and casualty books, are in WO 68. Militia attestation papers, 1806 to 1915, are in WO 96. Much relevant correspondence is in WO 50. For the period after 1815, little survives.

Militia records are invaluable sources. Military and economic historians can learn much from their enumerations of equipment, of the occupations of recruits, and of taxes and loans levied. Demographers may obtain at least minimal estimates of population. In Monmouthshire, they have been used to demonstrate the way in which Welsh patronymic surnames gradually developed.[28] Family historians can use them to trace surnames across entire counties.

Lord Lieutenants continued to hold a powerful office into the twentieth century. In 1838, it was said that 'if fires and riots grow alarming the Justices of the Peace wait for the Lord Lieutenant. He may be an aged or inactive man, or he may not be resident in the county, but till the Lord Lieutenant comes forward the magistrates do nothing collectively.'[29] As late as 1866, the Privy Council used the influence of Lord Lieutenants to encourage compliance with the controversial provisions of the Cattle Diseases Prevention Act 1866.[30] However, control of the Militia was removed from them in 1871, and the introduction of elected county councils in 1888 weakened their powers. Appointees increasingly became local worthies, rather than figures of national significance. Ceremonial functions gradually became their *raison d'être*, although they continued to nominate Justices of the Peace until 1910 (Clerks of the Peace in practice increasingly directed appointments),[31] and played important roles in raising forces during the First World War. They continue to represent the Queen to this day.

FURTHER READING

An introduction to the history of the Lieutenancy is provided by:
• Jebb, Miles, *The Lord-Lieutenants and their Deputies*. (Phillimore, 2007).

For the early Lieutenancy, see:
• Thomson, Gladys Scott. *Lords Lieutenants in the Sixteenth Century: A Study in Tudor Local Administration*. (Longmans Green & Co., 1923).

• Stater, Victor L. *Noble Government: the Stuart Lord Lieutenancy and the Transformation of English Politics.* (University of Georgia Press, 1994).

Deputy Lieutenants are discussed by:
• Thomson, Gladys Scott. 'The origin and growth of the office of deputy lieutenant', *Transactions of the Royal Historical Society* 4th series, 5, 1922, pp.150–67.

For the history of the Militia, see:
• Boynton, Lindsay. *The Elizabethan Militia, 1558-1638.* (David & Charles, 1971).
• Western, J.R. *The English Militia in the Eighteenth Century: the Story of a Political Issue, 1660-1802.* (Routledge & Kegan Paul, 1965).
• Fortescue, J.W. *The County Lieutenancies and the Army, 1803-1814.* (Macmillan, 1909).

The names of Lord Lieutenants are listed in:
• Sainty, J.C. *Lieutenants of Counties, 1585-1642.* (Bulletin of the Institute of Historical Research special supplement 8, 1970). Continued for 1660–1974 in *List and Index Society special series* 12, 1974.

The above discussion of surviving Militia lists and muster rolls draws heavily on two Gibson guides, which provide much greater detail, and list surviving records:
• Gibson, Jeremy, & Dell, Alan. *Tudor and Stuart Muster Rolls: a Directory of Holdings in the British Isles.* (Federation of Family History Societies, 1989).
• Gibson, Jeremy, & Medlycott, Mervyn. *Militia Lists and Musters 1757-1876: a Directory to Holdings in the British Isles.* (5th ed. Family History Partnership, 2013).

On the 1522 muster (in addition to the county volumes listed below), see:
• Cornwall, Julian. 'A Tudor domesday: the musters of 1522', *Journal of the Society of Archivists* 3(1), 1965, pp.19–24.
• Goring, J.L. 'The general proscription of 1522', *English Historical Review* 86(341), 1971, pp.681–705.

A detailed guide to Militia records, post-1757, is provided by:
- Spencer, William. *Records of the Militia & Volunteer Forces, 1757-1945, including Records of the Volunteers, Rifle Volunteers, Yeomanry, Imperial Yeomanry, Fencibles, Territorials, and the Home Guard.* (Rev ed. PRO Publications, 1997).

See also:
- Militia
  www.nationalarchives.gov.uk/help-with-your-research/research-guides/Militia
- British Army muster rolls and pay lists c.1730–1898
  www.nationalarchives.gov.uk/help-with-your-research/research-guides/british-army-muster-rolls-pay-lists-1730-1898

The following editions of Lieutenancy books, muster rolls, military surveys, etc., contain useful introductions:

Bedfordshire
- Lutt, Nigel, ed. *Bedfordshire Muster Rolls, 1539-1831: a Selection of Transcripts with Commentary.* (Publications of the Bedfordshire Historical Record Society 71, 1992).

Buckinghamshire
- Chibnall, A.C., ed. *The Certificates of Musters for Buckinghamshire in 1522.* (HMSO, 1973. Also published as Buckinghamshire Record Society 17, 1973).
- Beckett, Ian F.W., ed. *The Buckinghamshire Posse Comitatus 1798.* (Buckinghamshire Record Society 22, 1985).

Cambridgeshire
- Bourgeois, E.J., ed. *A Cambridgeshire Lieutenancy Letterbook, 1595-1605.* (Cambridgeshire Records Society 12, 1997).

Cornwall
- Stoate, T.L., ed. *The Cornwall Military Survey, 1522, with the Loan Books and a Tinners Muster Roll, c.1535.* (T.L. Stoate, 1987). Re-published on CD, B.D. Welchman, 2005. Searchable online at www.cornwall-opc-database.org/extra-searches/muster-rolls

- Douch, H.L., ed. *The Cornwall Muster Roll, 1569*. (T.L. Stoate, 1984). Republished on CD (B.D. Welchman, 2005). Re-published on CD, with returns for Somerset, Devon and Dorset, as *The West Country Muster: Somerset, Devon and Cornwall, 1569; Dorset 1539, 1542 and 1569*. (B.D. Welchman, 2005).

Cumberland
- Jarvis, Rupert C. *The Jacobite Risings of 1715 and 1745*. (Cumberland County Council record series 1, 1954). Records of the Lord Lieutenant and Quarter Sessions.

Devon *see also* Cornwall.
- Rowe, Margery M., ed. *Tudor Exeter: Tax Assessments 1489-1595, including the Military Survey 1522*. (Devon & Cornwall Record Society new series 22, 1977).
- Hoskins, W.G., ed. *Exeter Militia list 1803*. (Phillimore, 1972). Actually a *levée en masse* list.

Dorset *see* Cornwall.

Essex
- Quintrell, B.W., ed. *The Maynard Lieutenancy Book*. (Essex Historical Documents 3. Essex Record Office, 1993).

Gloucestershire
- Hoyle, R.W., ed. *The Military Survey of Gloucestershire, 1522*. (Gloucestershire Record Series 6, Bristol & Gloucestershire Archaeological Society, 1993).
- Smith, John. *Men and Armour for Gloucestershire in 1608*. (Alan Sutton, 1980).

Herefordshire
- Faraday, Michael, ed. *Herefordshire Militia Assessments 1663*. (Camden 4th series 10, Royal Historical Society, 1972), pp.29–185.

Hertfordshire
- King, Ann J., ed. *Muster Books for North & East Hertfordshire, 1580-1605*. (Hertfordshire Record Publications 12, 1996).

Kent
• Thomson, Gladys Scott. ed. *The Twysden Lieutenancy Papers, 1583-1668*. (Kent Archaeological Society Records Branch 10, 1926).

Lancashire
• Harland, John, ed. *The Lancashire Lieutenancy under the Tudors and Stuarts: the civil and military government of the county, as illustrated by a series of royal and other letters, orders of the Privy Council, the Lord Lieutenant, and other authorities, &c.,&c. chiefly derived from the Shuttleworth mss at Gawthorpe Hall, Lancashire*. (Chetham Society Old Series 49–50, 1859).
• 'Sir Roger Bradshaigh's letter-book'. *Historic Society of Lancashire and Cheshire* 63; New Series 27, 1911, pp.120–73. Bradshaigh served as Deputy Lieutenant.

Monmouthshire
• Hopkins, Tony, ed. *Men at Arms: Musters in Monmouthshire, 1539 and 1601-2*. (South Wales Record Society 21, 2009).

Norfolk
• Rye, Walter, ed. *State papers relating to musters, beacons, shipmoney &c in Norfolk, from 1626 chiefly to the beginning of the civil war*. (Norfolk & Norwich Archaeological Society, 1907).
• Dunn, Richard Minta, ed. *Norfolk Lieutenancy Journal, 1660-1676*. (Norfolk Record Society Publications 45, 1977). Continued by Cozens-Hardy, B., ed. *Norfolk Lieutenancy Journal, 1676-1701*. (Norfolk Record Society 30, 1961).

Northamptonshire
• Goring, Jeremy, & Wake, Joan, eds. *Northamptonshire Lieutenancy Papers and other Documents, 1580-1614*. (Northamptonshire Record Society Publications 27, 1975).
• Hatley, V.A. ed. *Northamptonshire Militia Lists, 1777*. (Northamptonshire Record Society Publications 25, 1973).
• Wake, J., ed. *The Montague Musters Book, 1602-1623*. (Northamptonshire Record Society Publications 7, 1935).
• Wake, Joan, ed. *A copy of papers relating to musters, beacons, subsidies, etc., in the county of Northampton, A.D. 1586-1623*. (Northamptonshire Record Society Publications 3, 1926).

Oxfordshire
- Beauchamp, Peter C., ed. *The Oxfordshire Muster Rolls, 1539, 1542, 1569.* (Oxfordshire Record Society 60, 1996).

Rutland
- Cornwall, J.C., ed. *Tudor Rutland: The County Community under Henry VIII: the Military Survey, 1522, and Lay Subsidy, 1524-5, for Rutland.* (Rutland Record Society 1, 1980).

Somerset *see also* Cornwall.
- Green, Emanuel, ed. *Certificate of Musters in the County of Somerset, temp Eliz., A.D. 1569.* (Somerset Record Society 20, 1904).

Suffolk
- Pound, John, ed. *The Military Survey of 1522 for Babergh Hundred.* (Suffolk Record Society 28, 1986).

Surrey
- Craib, T., ed. *Surrey Musters (taken from the Loseley mss).* (Surrey Record Society 3, 1919).

Wiltshire
- Murphy, W.P.D. ed. *The Earl of Hertford's Lieutenancy Papers, 1603-1612.* (Wiltshire Record Society 23, 1969).

Chapter 2

SHERIFFS

Sheriffs hold one of the oldest offices in English government. *The Anglo-Saxon Chronicle* records that, when Viking ships arrived at Portland in 787, the 'reeve', that is, the Sheriff, 'rode thither and tried to compel them to go to the royal manor, for he did not know what they were; and then they slew him'.[1] Anglo-Saxon and Norman Sheriffs were the King's bailiffs. They had charge of his castles and manors, oversaw defence, administered justice and collected the Crown's dues. The office was of fundamental importance to constitutional development in the eleventh and twelfth centuries.

Norman Sheriffs have had a bad press. Their extortions are frequently recorded in Domesday Book. Picot, Sheriff of Cambridgeshire, was described by the Abbot of Ely as 'a hungry lion, a ravening wolf, a cunning fox, a dirty pig and an impudent dog'. Their reputation under Norman and Angevin dynasties did not change. Robin Hood and the Sheriff of Nottingham were legendary, but the character of the latter showed what contemporaries thought of his office. In 1215, King John's Magna Carta reluctantly promised that 'We will appoint as justices, constables, Sheriffs, or other officials, only men that know the law of the realm and are minded to keep it well.'

Sheriffs were the prime arbiters of justice in the shires, although ecclesiastical causes were removed from their jurisdiction when ecclesiastical courts were created in 1072. Their powers were gradually whittled down, and subjected to fixed rules. In the twelfth and thirteenth centuries, they were subordinated financially to the Exchequer, and judicially to the central courts; coroners (see Chapter 11) kept an eye on them. After 1258, they served for one year only. Many shrieval abuses recorded in the 'ragman' rolls (National Archives, series SC 5) were uncovered in 1275.[2]

Sheriffs continued to represent the Crown in their counties, and to undertake extensive routine activities; in 1323–4, the Sheriff of Bedfordshire dealt with at least 2,000 writs.[3] But they ceased exercising substantial executive authority. Local landowners, rather than the nobility, increasingly held the office.

In the medieval period, the Sheriff's 'Tourn' sat regularly in each Hundred. It dealt with petty matters such as encroachments on the highways, trading offences and bridges out of repair. It supervised the work of Hundred Courts, hearing presentments of serious assaults and robberies, and holding View of Frankpledge. The View aimed to ensure that every man was a member of a tithing. Tithings were groups of ten or twelve men, required to produce in court any of their members who committed an offence. The tourn provided the bulk of the work for Justices of gaol delivery at Assizes until 1461, when the hearing of indictments was removed to Quarter Sessions. Thus began the Tourn's steady decline. By the seventeenth century, according to Dalton, the Tourn 'is now almost grown out of use'.[4]

Sheriffs nevertheless remained the principal representatives of the Crown in the counties until the mid-sixteenth century, and the secular officers best placed to enforce the Reformation. When Henry VIII broke with Rome in 1533, the Sheriffs were instructed to 'inform yourselves whether . . . the bishop executes our commands without veil or dissumulation'.[5] Paradoxically, the instruction was the prelude to decreasing shrieval powers. It was followed by the dissolution of the monasteries, which drastically reduced the revenues Sheriffs were expected to collect.[6] Duties relating to crown lands gradually passed to escheators, feodaries, and receivers. Shrieval military functions were lost to Commissioners of Musters, and subsequently Lord Lieutenants. At the end of the sixteenth century, William Harrison remarked that the shrievalty was reduced to dealing with 'such small matters as oft arise amongst the inferior sort of people'.[7]

Shrieval powers did increase under Charles I. Sheriffs compiled lists of wealthy landowners who could be distrained for knighthood.[8] Charles's 1630 Book of Orders (see Chapter 5) gave Sheriffs a coordinating role over social and economic policy, and supervisory powers over Justices of the Peace. However, shrieval attempts to collect Ship Money only succeeded in rousing virulent opposition, leading eventually to civil war. The powers bestowed by the Book of Orders were immediately lost, never to be regained. Parliament, however, granted other new powers. Sheriffs were expected to assist County Committees (see Chapter 13) and the hated Excise Commissioners; they raised money for the relief of distressed Protestants in Ireland, ensured that tithes were paid to clergy imposed by Parliament, were involved with the pre-sale surveys of Crown and Episcopal lands, and even received writs from the patrons of livings for the institution of new clergy.[9] These powers, too, were immediately lost on the Restoration of Charles II.

After 1660, Sheriffs continued undertaking much of the routine work of the courts, serving writs, empanelling juries, and executing judgements. Such work filled ninety pages in Dalton's *Officium Vicecomitum*, the contemporary guide to their duties. The Sheriff attended both Quarter Sessions and Assizes (see Chapters 5 and 12), acting as their chief executive officer, arranging accommodation for the Assize judges, providing dinner for the Justices, presenting calendars of prisoners, empanelling juries, and gaoling, whipping or hanging convicted prisoners. Writs directed to the Sheriff ordered him to proclaim the Sessions, to summon officers and juries, to bring offenders and suspects to court. Sheriffs also proclaimed statutes and ordinances in their County Courts, empanelled juries for coroners and escheators,[10] and continued to be able to call out the *posse comitatus* until the nineteenth century.

Sheriffs or their under-Sheriffs presided over county courts; the county's freeholders owing suit (the duty was attached to ownership of specific property) acted as judges and jurors, and determined much important litigation. These courts' long decline commenced in the thirteenth century, with cases increasingly being removed to superior courts. The prime evidence for their medieval activities is found in the records sent to those superior courts, and now in The National Archives. By the mid-fourteenth century, the central courts 'had appropriated almost every jurisdiction of significance from the county courts'.[11] By the sixteenth century, the latter were only hearing cases concerning the recovery of small debts. However, county courts continued to elect coroners (see Chapter 11) and Members of Parliament.

The Sheriff himself usually presided at Parliamentary elections, under a Chancery writ. County members were elected in his county court. Borough authorities presided over their own elections, although Sheriffs made returns of elections for them. Sheriffs were not supposed to stand themselves. They were frequently accused of returning members who had not been elected, of permitting unqualified persons to vote, and of closing polls prematurely whilst their friends were in the lead.

Between 1696 and 1872, Sheriffs compiled pollbooks recording the names and parishes of voters, sometimes their occupations, the nature of their qualification and their vote. The franchise in county constituencies was held after 1429 by freeholders who held land worth forty shillings per annum. Only those actually voting were recorded. Pollbooks survive in both print and manuscript. There is no consistency in the information they give, or in their arrangement. Voters may be listed alphabetically, by parish, or even by the order in which votes were cast. Occasionally, volumes were annotated; for example, a 1727 Bedfordshire pollbook records sales of property and deaths prior to the 1734 election.[12] They ceased when the secret ballot was introduced in 1867.

Major collections of pollbooks are available at the Institute of Historical Research, Guildhall Library, the British Library, and the Society of Genealogists, as well as in local studies libraries and record offices. Many can be searched online search.ancestry.co.uk/search/db.aspx?dbid=2410. Pollbooks are invaluable sources for political and social historians, and enable genealogists to trace the homes of family names across entire counties. Published lists of surviving pollbooks are noted below.

The judicial functions of County Courts were moribund by the eighteenth century. Courts of Request dealing with petty debt business replaced them in many boroughs. Debt business was taken over by new County Courts in 1846 (see Chapter 13); these were not, however, the old courts reformed. The latter were not formally abolished until 1977.

Technically, it continued to be the Sheriff's duty to preserve the peace, although in practice most of his duties were exercised by Justices and the Lieutenancy by c.1600. Similarly, although he remained titular keeper of the county gaol, the Sheriff was rarely involved in its administration. Most shrieval duties were exercised by deputy. On appointment, the Sheriff himself appointed an under-Sheriff, a clerk for his court, and Hundred Bailiffs. They had frequently held office under his predecessor. Under-Sheriffs could exercise all shrieval functions, and frequently represented them on the Bench and at the Exchequer. Even in the thirteenth-century,

Sheriffs usually had at least four clerks.[13] Hundred Bailiffs executed writs, collected the Crown's debts, and summoned juries.[14] Attorneys were appointed to represent Sheriffs in the central courts.

These officers had plenty of opportunity for corruption. Tampering with jury lists, extorting fees from witnesses, and other nefarious practices were common. Bailiffs purchased their office from the Sheriff, and needed enough money to pay for it. The unreliability and dishonesty of Sheriffs' officers was arguably 'the chief weakness in English local government during the Stuart period'.[15] At least one-third of early seventeenth-century Wiltshire bailiffs were the subject of complaints made to courts.[16] Paradoxically, although the Sheriff's tenure had been limited to one year in order to reduce shrieval corruption, in practice, annual office rendered nugatory any attempt by him to control the corruption of his subordinates. Sheriffs could nevertheless be held liable for their actions, and subjected to expensive litigation.

Sheriffs collected fines and amercements imposed by Quarter Sessions, Assizes and the Westminster courts. They also collected some taxes, and revenue from the Crown's estates. Until 1788, monies received, after deduction of expenses such as the entertainment of Assize judges, the costs of poor prosecutors (from 1752), and rewards to informers, were paid into the Exchequer. Court officials compiled estreats (abstracts) of fines for the Exchequer, which in turn issued a 'summons of the green wax' to the Sheriff to collect and pay in the amounts due. Summonses are in The National Archives, series E 382.

Quarter Sessions estreats were written in duplicate and indented by the Clerk of the Peace, one copy for the Exchequer, the other for the Sheriff. They indicate the dates and places of sittings, list crown revenues, and name Clerks of the Peace and active Justices (thus providing one means of tracing these officers). Estreats sent to the Exchequer are now in The National Archives, series E 137 and E 362 (with a few in E 389). Those given to the Sheriff may sometimes be found amongst Quarter Sessions records, as well as in E 137.[17] Estreats from many Westminster courts are also in E 137. Those prepared by Clerks of Assize are in E 362, and in various ASSI series. Many other National Archives series also include estreats.

At the end of his year of office, the Sheriff received a 'summons of the Pipe', to bring in his accounts. Some are in E 389. The pipe rolls (E 372), running from the twelfth century until 1832, record them. Many

early rolls have been published by the Pipe Roll Society www.piperollsociety.co.uk. For brief introductions to their study, see:
• Crook, David. 'Pipe rolls', in Thompson, K.M., ed. *Short Guides to Records Second Series 25-48*. (Historical Association, 1997), pp.75–8.
• Medieval Financial Records: Pipe rolls, 1130–c.1300. www.nationalarchives.gov.uk/help-with-your-research/research-guides/medieval-financial-records-pipe-rolls-1130-1300/

The procedure by which pipe rolls were drawn up is described in:
• *Introduction to the Study of the Pipe Rolls*. (Pipe Roll Society 3, 1884).

Medieval pipe rolls have been much studied. However, later rolls deserve more attention. Between 1581 and 1591, they record the fines and forfeitures inflicted on recusants. Early seventeenth century rolls list arrears of Ship Money.

A variety of other shrieval financial documents are in The National Archives, series E 389. These include accounts, returns of 'illeviable debts', vouchers relating to the cost of hangings, whippings, the pillory and other punishments, petitions for allowances, and various other documents. Other records (especially those of county courts) are not well preserved, although shrieval activities can be traced amongst the records of all the courts.

Assize judges, and later Lord Lieutenants, played important roles in identifying potential Sheriffs. The Lord Chancellor presented the King with a list of three possible candidates for each county;[18] he, with a stylus, ceremoniously 'pricked' the ones he selected. Charles I sometimes chose malcontents in order to exclude them from the House of Commons. When he wanted Ship Money collected he chose men prepared to collect it. During the Interregnum, local Members of Parliament identified those eligible to serve, and appointment was made by ordinance of Parliament. In the 1680s, political turmoil led the Crown to make very careful choice of reliable Royalists.

Service if 'pricked' was compulsory. The office became an expensive honour; its holder had to be a gentleman of wealth. Quite apart from hospitality for Assize judges, dinners for Justices and the cost of expensive ceremonial, Sheriffs had to pay substantial fees to take up office, and to settle their accounts. It was not until 1717 that fees were regulated by statute, and that provision was made for Sheriffs to be re-imbursed. Sir Richard Cholmley of Whitby is said to have spent £1,000 on his 1624 shrievalty, much of it on litigation.[19] The holder of the office could neither leave the county, nor become a Member of Parliament, during his year of office. Sheriffs could not act as Justices (although many ignored this provision).

Attitudes to holding office varied: many were reluctant to take on the expense or the onerous duties. Some, however, seized the chance to enhance their own reputations, or to pursue their own interests. In Norfolk, bitter divisions within the gentry led to vigorous competition for office in the 1590s; it offered substantial opportunities to subvert court processes in factional interests.

The Sheriffs' rolls pricked by the Crown are in The National Archives, series C 227, C 172, and PC 3. They are described in:
- Wilson, Jean S. 'Sheriffs' rolls of the sixteenth and seventeenth centuries', *English Historical Review* 47(185), 1932, pp.31–45.

Appointments of Sheriffs are recorded on the patent rolls (C66). On appointment, Sheriffs entered recognizances binding themselves to perform the duties of their office, under pain of a monetary penalty. Registers of recognizances from 1488 are in E 165. Names can also be found on the pipe rolls, and in many of the sources mentioned above. For a full list, see:
- *List of Sheriffs for England and Wales from the earliest times to 1831, compiled from documents in the Public Record Office*. Lists and indexes 9. (HMSO, 1896).

For Norman Sheriffs, see:
- Green, Judith A. *English Sheriffs to 1154*. Public Record Office handbook 24. (HMSO, 1990).

More recent appointees are listed in the *London Gazette*, www.thegazette.co.uk/browse-publications. Numerous county lists of Sheriffs have been published; many are also available online. Appointments of under-Sheriffs are recorded in The National Archives, series E 389.

FURTHER READING
Sheriffs are introduced in:
- Gladwin, Irene. *The Sheriff: the Man and his Office*. (Victor Gollancz, 1974).

There are a number of works covering particular periods. These include:

- Morris, William A. *The Medieval English Sheriff to 1300*. (Manchester University Press, 1927).
- Gorski, Richard. *The Fourteenth-Century Sheriff: English Local Administration in the Late Middle Ages*. (Boydell Press, 2003).
- Karraker, C.H. *The Seventeenth-Century Sheriff: a Comparative Study of the Sheriff in England and the Chesapeake Colonies, 1607-1689*. (University of North Carolina Press, 1930).

Contemporary legal handbooks include:
- Dalton, Michael. *Officium Vicecomitum: the office and authority of Sheriffs*. (Richard & Edward Atkins, 1582).
- Hale, Matthew. *A Short Treatise touching Sheriffs' Accompts*. (Will Shrowsbury, 1683).
- Atkinson, George. *Sherriff Law, or, a practical treatise on the office of Sheriff, unde-Sheriff, bailiff, etc*. (3rd ed. Longman, Brown, Green & Longmans, 1854).

On the county court, see:
- Morris, William Alfred. *The Early English County Court: an Historical Treatise with Illustrative Documents*. (University of California Press, 1926).
- Palmer, Robert C. *The County Courts of Medieval England, 1150-1350*. (Princeton University Press, 1982).

Pollbooks are listed by:
- Gibson, Jeremy, & Rogers, Colin. *Poll Books, 1696-1872: a directory to holdings in Great Britain*. (4th ed. Family History Partnership, 2008).
- Sims, J. *A Handlist of British Parliamentary Poll Books*. (University of Leicester History Dept occasional paper 4, 1984).

Published local records used here include:
Bedfordshire
- Fowler, G. Herbert, ed. *Rolls from the Office of the Sheriff of Beds and Bucks., 1332-1334*. (Quarto Memoirs of the Bedfordshire Historical Record Society 3, 1929).
- Collett-White, James, ed. *How Bedfordshire Voted, 1685-1735: the evidence of local poll books*. (Publications of the Bedfordshire Historical Record Society 85 & 87, 2006–8. Continued for 1735–84 in vol. 90, 2011).

Buckinghamshire *see* Bedfordshire.

Lancashire
• Ffarington, Susan Maria, ed. *The Farington Papers: the Shrievalty of William Ffarington, esq., A.D. 1636 . . ..* (Chetham Society old series 39, 1856).

Nottinghamshire
• *Poll-Books of Nottingham and Nottinghamshire, 1710.* (Thoroton Society record series 18, 1958).

Chapter 3

JUSTICES OF THE PEACE

The work of Lord Lieutenants and Sheriffs was closely intertwined with that of Justices of the Peace (frequently referred to as Magistrates after c.1800). Their offices helped them create a sense of community and exclusiveness within the landed classes which differentiated them from the lower orders. They were convinced that they could provide better county government than uninformed, and potentially interfering, oppressive and exploitative, outsiders. Central government was not convinced; Lord Burghley was constantly frustrated by the poor quality of many Justices. But a paid bureaucracy was unaffordable. The strength of English government was built upon the unpaid services of the landed gentry.

Justices sitting in Quarter Sessions ruled their counties for more than half a millennia. As James I put it, they were 'the King's eyes and ears in the country'. And, even if the Assize judges were 'never so careful and industrious, if the Justices of the Peace under them put not their helping hands, in vain is all their labour'.[1]

Justices of the Peace had a three-fold responsibility: they preserved the peace, administered their counties, and acted as arbitrators. Crime was their original *raison d'être*, and their evolving practice probably had a greater effect upon the development of criminal law than either statute or the influence of professional lawyers. Keepers of the Peace, as Justices of the Peace were originally known, were first commissioned by Richard I in 1195. Their primary role was to arrest suspects, and to inquire into felonies and trespasses. Their powers were steadily widened;[2] they became Conservators of the Peace in 1327 (the Statute of Westminster), and Justices of the Peace in 1361. In the fourteenth century they began to try indictments, and acquired jurisdiction over economic matters such as prices and wages, and weights and measures. In the sixteenth century, Parliament gradually transferred shrieval criminal jurisdiction to Justices of the Peace, making the Sheriff merely their executive agent. The Tudors added greatly to Justices' workloads – 'not loads, but stacks of statutes', in the much-quoted words of William Lambarde. He estimated in 1602 that there were 309 statutes bearing on their activities, of which 176 had been passed since 1485.[3] Religious observance, alehouses and bridges, were just three of the matters they supervised. The Elizabethan Poor Laws (see Chapter 8) were perhaps the heaviest 'stacks' they had to bear; these took up much of their time for the following two centuries. Eighteenth-century Parliaments added to individual Justices' workloads by sharply increasing the number of criminal matters they could deal with summarily.

Justices' powers were reduced in the nineteenth century. Their ability to follow their own inclinations was greatly restricted by reforms of court procedures. The 1834 New Poor Law Act transferred powers to the newly-created guardians (although Justices were *ex officio* guardians themselves). County police forces took over the role of collecting evidence for prosecution of offenders. In 1888, the Local Government Act 1888 created county councils, and deprived Quarter Sessions of all their administrative powers. The judicial activities of Justices of the Peace continue to this day, but the 1888 Act marks the end of the period covered by this book.

These changes were accompanied by an increasing flow of printed manuals advising Justices on their powers. William Lambarde's *Eirenarcha* went through twelve editions between 1581 and 1619. Michael Dalton's *The Country Justice* went through ten editions between 1618 and 1661, and continued to be in print throughout the eighteenth century. Richard Burn's *The Justice of the Peace and Parish Officer* went through no less than thirty editions between 1755 and 1869, and served as the standard work in the early nineteenth century. Stone's *Justices' Manual* has been regularly updated (under various titles) since 1842, and is still authoritative. The journal *Justice of the Peace*, first published in 1837, also includes much useful information. These and other manuals are still invaluable guides to the contemporary work of Justices of the Peace.[4]

Under Acts of 1388 and 1390, Justices were entitled to be paid four shillings per day for attendance at Quarter Sessions. They could also be paid five shillings per day for divisional meetings under the Statute of Artificers of 1563. Payments were regularly recorded on the pipe rolls.

THE

Justice of the Peace,

AND

PARISH OFFICER.

By RICHARD BURN, LL.D.

LATE CHANCELLOR OF THE DIOCESE OF CARLISLE.

THE TWENTY-THIRD EDITION:

With CORRECTIONS, ADDITIONS, and IMPROVEMENTS.
The CASES brought down to the End of Easter Term,
1 GEO. IV. 1820.
And the STATUTES to the 1 GEO. IV. 1820.

By GEORGE CHETWYND, ESQ. M.P.

BARRISTER AT LAW,

AND CHAIRMAN OF THE GENERAL QUARTER SESSIONS OF THE PEACE
FOR THE COUNTY OF STAFFORD.

Dr. Burn has great merit: He has done great service, and deserves great
commendation. *Per* Lord MANSFIELD C. J.   Burr. S. C. 548.

IN FIVE VOLUMES.

VOL. I.

LONDON:

Printed by A. STRAHAN, Law-Printer to the King's Most Excellent Majesty:
For T. CADELL and W. DAVIES, in the Strand;
F. C. & J. RIVINGTON, St. Paul's Church-Yard, & Waterloo-Place;
JOSEPH BUTTERWORTH and Son, Fleet-Street;
and LONGMAN, HURST, REES, ORME, and BROWN,
Paternoster-Row.
1820.

Burns' The Justice of the Peace *was the leading handbook for the eighteenth and nineteenth-century Justices.*

31

Peers and ecclesiastics could not claim, although the names of the former are noted. Justices were also entitled to levy a wide variety of fees. Constables wanting to be sworn in, overseers who wanted their accounts allowed, everyone bound by recognizance, all had to pay a fee.

The powers given to Justices were set out in their Commissions, which were re-modelled in 1590, and remained virtually unchanged until 1878.[5] Individual justices were empowered to act as conservators of the peace; the justices collectively were empowered to hold sessions and to judge felonies, trespasses, and misdemeanours. They were to leave *casus difficultatis* (difficult causes – in practice, most felonies) to the Assize judges. The *Custos Rotulorum* was instructed to bring all writs, precepts, processes and indictments to the sessions for determination.[6] The Lord Chancellor headed each Commission, followed by other members of the council, the Assize judges, the local nobility, and, finally, the knights and gentlemen. Those who were 'of the quorum', that is, supposedly had legal training, were identified. Some of them always had to be present during sessions.

In a status-conscious society, the order in which Justices were listed was important: it determined their seating order, and therefore their status, at both Quarter Sessions and Assizes. Thomas Lovell spent £40 in 1598 to 'be restored to his former position in the Commission' for Norfolk.[7] In the eighteenth century, the importance of such distinctions diminished; from 1753, Justices were named alphabetically – apart from the increasing number of clerics, who were named at the end.

The appointment of Justices of the Peace was the responsibility of the Lord Chancellor,[8] although members of the Privy Council, and the Assize judges, were automatically appointed. Before the Civil War, Assize judges were expected to nominate candidates. They tried to ensure that some members of the Bench had legal training, and that no area was devoid of Justices. 'When any desireth to be a justice, he getteth a certificate from divers Justices of the Peace in the county, to the Justices of Assize, certifying them of their sufficiency and ability.'[9] Recommendations also came from elsewhere. In 1564 and 1587, the bishops were asked to recommend 'well affected' gentlemen for appointment. They did not always wait for invitations to make recommendations. Local magnates also had influence. In Somerset, John Poulett secured several appointments in the 1620s through the Duke of Buckingham.[10] In Norfolk, the Duke of Norfolk probably influenced seventeen of the thirty-two appointments to the Bench made between 1558 and 1572.[11] Lord Chancellor Ellesmere caused consternation when he announced in 1605 that he only intended to make appointments on the recommendation of Assize judges. The patronage network at court defeated his intention.[12]

During the Interregnum, the security of what many saw as an illegitimate regime was a major issue. That resulted in the nomination of serving army and naval officers as Justices. Thirteen officers were serving as Justices in Hampshire in 1652. Officers of the Restoration navy also served on the Hampshire Bench.[13]

After the Restoration, Lord Lieutenants increasingly assumed supervisory powers over the Bench. From the mid-eighteenth century nominations were increasingly left to them. By 1828, Brougham could comment that 'such a thing is hardly known as any interference with respect to these nominations by the Lord Chancellor. He looks to the Lord Lieutenant . . . for the names of proper persons.'[14] Lieutenants in turn sought advice from Clerks of the Peace, chairmen of Quarter Sessions and other leading Justices. Kent's Lord Lieutenant insisted on hearing the advice of the Justices in the Division where the nominee resided, on the basis that they would have to work with the new appointee.

Most of the actual work was done by prominent gentlemen, or perhaps by clerics. Lords of the Council never appeared at Quarter Sessions and Lord Lieutenants rarely put in an appearance. Local aristocrats were usually absent, at least until the early nineteenth century, when many took prominent roles. Most gentlemen aspired to be Justices of the Peace. Office enabled them to protect their adherents, attack those of opposing interests, and greatly augmented their ability to influence Parliamentary elections. It was their duty to preserve the peace, but they used their discretion to determine in whose interests the peace would be kept. Not all Justices were entirely peaceful: three members of the Shropshire Bench were indicted before their own Bench in 1414.[15] Nicholas Bacon complained in 1565 that many gentry wanted the office 'to serve the private affection of themselves and their friends as in overthrowing an old enemy or maintaining a friend, a servant or tenant'.[16]

In the seventeenth century, most Justices were pre-eminent in their neighbourhoods. In the eighteenth and nineteenth centuries, however, many new Justices gained more prestige from the office than they brought to it. Many sought local prestige from their position, rather than 'the trouble of doing the duty', as Lord Cowper put it.[17] That had always been the case. Assize judges frequently complained of those who neglected to swear their oaths. In Surrey, almost 50 per cent of recognizances issued between 1661 and 1663 were signed by just three of the fifty-one Justices.[18]

The proportion of Justices attending Quarter Sessions declined over the centuries. In the early fifteenth-century East Riding, attendance averaged 67 per cent.[19] During the late sixteenth century, between six and twelve attended the Wiltshire Quarter Sessions, although there could be as many as thirty or forty in the Commission.[20] James I issued a proclamation requiring Justices to attend Quarter Sessions. Clerks of the Peace were instructed to record their attendance, and to report non-attenders to the Lord Chancellor through the Assize judges.[21] Nothing changed. Two centuries later, perhaps half of the names on any Commission were those of merely titular Justices, who had never taken their oaths. The Merioneth Clerk of the Peace complained in 1800 that sessions were being lost due to the non-attendance of magistrates – despite the fact that there were about 150 in the county.[22]

Attendance at Quarter Sessions was only one measure of Justices' assiduity. Many who did not attend were nevertheless active locally. They heard the complaints of their neighbours, determined settlement cases, took recognizances, committed prisoners to gaol until the next Sessions, and undertook all the other out-of-sessions work which will be discussed in Chapter 4. More conscientious Justices could find office time-consuming. In Somerset, William Capell bitterly complained that 'it is sessions with me every day all the day long here, and I have no time for my own occasions, hardly to put meat into my mouth, and to add this of the subsidy is unmerciful'.[23]

The number of Justices in Commissions of the Peace gradually increased. A statute of 1388 limited their number in any one county to six, but this was ignored. In Gloucestershire, there were an average of 21.4 names in Commissions between 1461 and 1470, but 39.5 between 1497 and 1509.[24] The Elizabethan Privy Council tried to reduce numbers, with little success. In 1580, there were 1,738 justices for the whole country.[25] There were about 3,000 by the end of the seventeenth century (including those serving in boroughs), but only about 800 active at any one time.[26] By 1762, Gloucestershire had no less than 262 Justices,[27] although only a small percentage attended Sessions.

Justices of the Peace were appointed collectively by the Crown for the life of the monarch, or until the issue of a new Commission. New Commissions named the whole Bench, rather than individual justices. They were issued irregularly, superseding previous Commissions; Justices not named ceased to be Justices. Gloucestershire received sixty-one Commissions between 1461 and 1509; Cumberland only had fifteen in the same period.[28]

Certain qualifications were required. From 1439, Justices were expected to hold freehold land valued at more than £20 per annum. In the seventeenth century, they had to be 'of the most sufficient knights, esquires and gentlemen of the law' resident within the county.[29] In 1732, the qualification for appointment was increased to possession of land worth £100 per annum. Heirs to estates valued at over £300 became qualified in 1745.

Justices appointed to be 'of the quorum' were supposed to have some legal qualification, so that they could provide legal advice to their fellow justices. Under Elizabeth, the proportion of members of the quorum to the numbers of working justices rose from about one-third to about three-quarters.[30] Gentlemen were seeking the status, rather than educating themselves in the law. By the late seventeenth century, most Justices were 'of the quorum'.[31] The legal importance of the quorum was effectively abolished in 1753.

The only other post-Reformation requirements for appointment were to receive the sacrament from a Church of England clergyman, to take the oaths of allegiance and supremacy, and to subscribe to a declaration against transubstantiation (the belief that wine and bread became the Lord's flesh and blood when consecrated). Roman Catholics and, after 1662, Nonconformists, were excluded – although that did not prevent sympathisers from serving. Under James II, these requirements were relaxed; by 1688, perhaps 24 per cent of Justices were Roman Catholics, although they were dismissed after the Glorious Revolution.[32] Quarter Sessions papers record many oaths and subscriptions.

Before a new Justice could act, he had to take out his '*dedimus potestatem*', that is, take his oaths, and pay his fees. When William Hunt joined the Bench in 1744, he paid 1s 6d for his sacrament certificate,[33] £3-13s 6d for 'my *dedimus potestatum*', 10s 6d to Mr Salmon 'for his trouble in taking it [the *dedimus*] out', 2s to the Clerk of the Peace for being sworn in court, and 10s 6d for his 'colt-ale' (conviviality paid for by new Justices).[34] Assize judges frequently complained about Justices who neglected to swear their oaths.

There were also social qualifications which, when they were ignored, caused much debate in Parliament, and sometimes dissension on the Bench. The consensus of opinion was expressed by Mr Glascock in the 1601 House of Commons:

> I hold this for a ground infallible – that no poor man ought to be in authority. My reason is this: he will so bribe you and extort you, that the sweet scent of riches and gain taketh away and confoundeth the true taste of justice and equity . . . justice is never imprisoned or suppressed but by bribery.[35]

Glascock's comments could legitimately have been applied to eighteenth-century Middlesex. There, it was not easy to find suitable gentlemen prepared to take on the caseload facing urban Justices. In their absence, the government was forced to rely on 'trading justices', who sought the fees Justices could levy. Most were men of obscure origin, regarded with suspicion. In 1780, Burke described the Middlesex Bench as 'the scum of the earth . . . some of whom were notoriously men of such infamous characters that they are unworthy of any employ whatever, and others so ignorant that they could scarcely write their own names'.[36] Such Justices trod a thin dividing line between outright corruption and simply being over-active. They could easily demand payment for licencing 'disorderly houses' which should have been suppressed, or for ignoring prostitutes who should have been arrested. Quarrels amongst neighbours could be stirred up, allowing Justices to take recognizances from the disputants to keep the peace, and then release them from their bonds, whilst pocketing the fees these two actions permitted.

In the Provinces, corruption was limited. There were, admittedly, many 'sensual and ignorant small squires', guilty of 'oppressing their tenants, tyrannising over the neighbourhood, cheating the vicar, talking nonsense and getting drunk at sessions'.[37] But most rural Justices had no need for their fees, and did not seek to act arbitrarily or oppressively.

They were, however, exclusive, and unwilling to allow the lower orders to participate in government. When a mere grocer and Wesleyan Methodist was appointed to the Merionethshire Bench in 1833, his fellow Justices refused to work with him.[38] Tradesmen appointed to the Bench needed to be sufficiently wealthy to have put trade behind them. If they were, they could achieve social equality with the gentry. The Gloucestershire gentry demonstrated their acceptance of one wealthy clothier by electing him as chairman of the Bench.

Wealthy clergy were also regarded as the social equals of the gentry. Bishops were usually to be found in the Commission of the Peace, being first appointed in 1424. Occasionally, Deans of Cathedrals also served. Before the Reformation, a few heads of religious houses were appointed. Few other medieval clergy were either wealthy or educated. Between 1550 and 1800, clergy wealth and status increased dramatically. The gentry acquired many advowsons formerly held by monasteries; they used them to employ younger members of their family who had the Oxbridge degrees now required by Protestantism. And the enclosure movement dramatically increased the value of many parochial livings. Their incumbents had the status, and were increasingly appointed to the Bench. By c.1800, the more educated, aware and diligent members of the Bench were clergy. In many counties clergy served as chairmen. Indeed, the leading manual for Justices, Richard Burn's *The Justice of the Peace and Parish Officer* (1755; 30th edition, 1869) was written by the clerical chairman of the Westmorland Bench. Cobbett complained that many parochial incumbents were 'better known as Justices of the Peace than as clergymen'.[39] By the 1830s, clergy constituted about a quarter of England's justices. That was their high point; numbers declined to 6.1 per cent of the total in 1887.[40]

At the same time, a new type of Justice began to appear: the industrialist. By the mid-nineteenth century, 50 per cent of appointees in the Black Country were coal and iron masters.[41] Their emergence marked the beginning of the end of gentry dominance of Quarter Sessions, although their numbers were much greater in industrial boroughs which had their own Quarter Sessions. Overall, only 14.9 per cent of the county magistracy were from the middle classes in 1887.[42]

Justices remained on the Bench until they either died, or were excluded from a new Commission. Exclusion was uncommon, except for political reasons. The Duke of Somerset's 1548 re-modelling of the Devon and Cornwall Commissions removed traditionalist Justices who might have been able to prevent the Prayer Book rebellion in 1549. Charles I issued no less than 133 new Commissions in 1630.[43] Both Charles II and James II conducted significant purges during the 1680s – the latter in order to make room for Roman Catholics. Political purges continued throughout the early eighteenth century, but ceased entirely when Lord Hardwicke became Lord Chancellor in 1737.

Despite purges, exclusion was frequently temporary. The Crown could not afford to dismiss Justices, even when they actively opposed its policy. Lord Burghley's many attempts to remodel the Bench under Elizabeth failed: those he sought to exclude repeatedly crept back in.[44] Even in 1637, when many Sheriffs, Deputy Lieutenants, and Justices of the Peace refused to collect Ship Money, all Charles I could do was to threaten dismissal. He was unable to carry through the threat.[45] During the Interregnum, the Protectorate looked to the Justices for grudging acquiescence in its rule, rather than positive loyalty.

SOURCES

'There are lies, damned lies, and Commissions of the Peace'. Such was the tongue-in-cheek verdict on sources for Justices of the Peace by the compiler of an extensive listing for Wales.[46] A variety of different sources are available, although none now provide comprehensive coverage, and all are either prone to error, or liable to mislead if not treated cautiously. Ideally, researchers should consult several of the sources mentioned below.

Commissions of the Peace were the one source which had legal validity, and are always precisely dated. Commissions are now amongst Quarter Sessions records in local record offices, if they have survived. They tended to be ephemeral documents, frequently renewed. Whenever a new Justice was appointed, or an old one dismissed, a new Commision was issued – except in the case of death.

When a new Commission reached the Clerk of the Peace, he summoned new members of the Bench to take their oaths at the next Assizes, notified former Justices that their services were no longer required, and drew up lists of *nomina ministrorum* for both Assizes and Quarter Sessions. These listed all the officers expected to appear in court, including Justices of the Peace, coroners, escheators, Hundred Bailiffs, High Constables and others. Deaths of Justices are recorded. They were compiled for every session of both courts, and are the only lists of Justices of the Peace prepared at regular intervals directly from Commisions. *Nomina ministrorum* from Quarter Sessions are now in local record offices; those drawn up for Assizes are in The National Archives, frequently used as wrappers for the indictment files in ASSI series. Many compiled for the Welsh Court of Great Sessions are now in the National Library of Wales.

Commissions of the Peace should have been enrolled on the patent rolls (National Archives, series C 66). Justices paid a fee for enrolment. In practice, enrolment was done carelessly or perhaps not at all. There are none for the Welsh counties between 1564 and 1594. Sometimes, the information entered is misleading. Commissions for each regnal year were entered in alphabetical order, beginning with the Commission for Bedfordshire, which was dated. The dates for other Commissions were given as *ut supra* – 'as above'. This is incorrect: the Bedfordshire date has no relation to the dates of other counties' Commissions. Commissions were also sometimes entered on the roll for a regnal year which did not cover the date they were issued. The same Commission was also frequently entered on two successive patent rolls. Patent rolls cannot be relied on for dates. Nor are they necessarily reliable guides to the names in Commissions. Commissions were sent out long before the rolls were written. Rolls were therefore probably copied from Crown Office entry books (National Archives, series C 193/12-13; for 1601–73, see C 181), not the Commissions themselves. Entry books were regularly kept up to date as new Justices were added to Commissions, and old ones died or were dismissed. Consequently, the names on the patent rolls do not necessarily match the names in particular Commissions.

Copies of the Crown Office entry books, known as *libri pacis*, were distributed to other government agencies, such as the Privy Council and the Treasury. These were not updated as regularly as their exemplars, and were frequently discarded when their useful life was ended. They can be found in various National Archives series, for example, C 192, C 220, E 163, and amongst the State Papers. Some may also be found amongst private collections in institutions such as the British Library and Cambridge University Library.

The Crown Office also kept docket books recording the dates on which Commissions and other instruments under the great seal were issued. These record the names on the Commission, and also indicate names added or removed from the previous Commission, sometimes with reasons. They do not, however, record deaths of Justices. Docket books are in The National Archives, series C 231/1-8.

The Lord Chancellor made changes to Commissions by sending a fiat (an order) to the Crown Office. These fiats, dating from 1672 to 1974 (National Archives, C 234), record virtually all changes in Commissions. From the late 1730s, they frequently directed that names should be added to a Commission, rather than that a new Commission should be issued. Such Commissions could remain in force for many years.

Individual appointments for the period 1682–1974 are also recorded in fiats recommending appointments (National Archives C 364), which were checked and approved in the Chancellor's office, and sent to the Clerk of the Crown for entry in new Commissions. Fiats for the removal of Justices can be found with them.

Justices of the Peace are also named in the *London Gazette* (www.the gazette.co.uk/browse-publications), in the nineteenth century series of *Returns of Justices of the Peace* included in the Parliamentary papers, and in a wide range of other sources. Their attendance at Quarter Sessions is recorded in order books (see Chapter 5), in estreats sent to the Exchequer, and in the pipe rolls (see Chapter 2). Their signatures can be found on many of the documents which will be considered in subsequent chapters.

FURTHER READING
For a useful introduction, see:
• Moir, Esther. *The Justice of the Peace*. (Penguin, 1969).

The history of Justices from a legal point of view is recounted in the extensive:
• Skyrme, Sir Thomas. *History of the Justices of the Peace*. (3rd ed. Barry Rose, 1991).

The origins of the office are discussed by:
• Putnam, Bertha Haven. 'Transformation of the Keepers of the Peace into the Justices of the Peace 1327-1380', *Transactions of the Royal Historical Society* 4th Series 12, 1929, pp.19–48.
• Harding, Alan. 'The origins and early history of the Keepers of the Peace', *Transactions of the Royal Historical Society* 5th Series 10, 1960, pp.85–109.

• Verduyn, Anthony. 'The selection and appointment of Justices of the Peace in 1338', *Bulletin of the Institute of Historical Research* 68(165), 1995, pp.1–25.

For later periods, see:
• Lander, J.R. *English Justices of the Peace, 1461-1509*. (Alan Sutton, 1989).
• Gleason, J.H. *The Justices of the Peace in England, 1558 to 1640: a later eirenarcha*. (Clarendon Press, 1969). This includes many lists of JPs for Kent, Northamptonshire, Somerset, Worcestershire and the North Riding of Yorkshire in its appendices.
• Landau, Norma. *The Justices of the Peace, 1679-1760*. (University of California Press, 1984).
• Glassey, Lionel K.J. *Politics and the Appointment of Justices of the Peace, 1675-1720*. (Oxford University Press, 1979).

The introductions to a number of published Quarter Sessions rolls (listed in Chapter 5) also give useful information.

For a detailed guide to sources for Justices, see:
• Barnes, Thomas G., & Smith, A. Hassell. 'Justices of the Peace from 1558 to 1688: a revised list of sources', *Bulletin of the Institute of Historical Research* 32, 1959, pp.221–42.

For the Lord Chancellor's fiats, see:
• Glassey, L.K.J., and Landau, Norma. 'The Commission of the peace in the eighteenth century: a new source', *Bulletin of the Institute of Historical Research* 45, 1972, pp.247–65.

Welsh Justices are fully listed in:
• Phillips, J.R.S. *The Justices of the Peace in Wales and Monmouthshire, 1541 to 1689*. (University of Wales Press, 1975). This includes a valuable introduction.

Chapter 4

JUSTICES OF THE PEACE OUT OF SESSION

Before the nineteenth century, most of the work of individual Justices was done out of Sessions, either sitting on their own, or with one or two others. The lone Justice was the first port of call for complainants. The many cases brought before them by the poor indicate that the latter expected at least a modicum of justice: servants accused their employers of withholding wages, apprentices accused their masters of ill treatment, paupers sought relief from the parish. Vagrants, thieves, poachers and mere drunkards were brought before Justices by parish constables. Unemployed labourers were ordered to find masters; paupers were removed to their parish of settlement; vagrants were punished.

The single justice heard allegations, interviewed complainants and witnesses, examined the accused and determined whether there was evidence warranting appearance at Quarter Sessions. He could instigate inquiries, issue warrants and prepare indictments. Those who came before him could be 'encouraged' to 'volunteer' for service in the army or navy, and thus avoid formal prosecutions. One of his most potent weapons was the power to demand that a person enter into a recognizance (discussed below).

The Justice might be asked to sign overseers' accounts, to approve nominations of overseers, and to issue certificates of various sorts. Sometimes, he took part in campaigns against particular social 'vices', such as church ales, profane swearing and non-attendance at church. His powers over the sale of staple commodities, such as bread and ale, meant he could forestall disturbances by ensuring that sufficient food was available in times of shortage or famine. He could arrange for orphans to be looked after, ensure the equitable administration of poor relief and resolve disputes between neighbours.

ARBITRATION

The informal arbitration Justices provided was highly valued by their communities. Quarter Sessions frequently referred disputes to individual Justices to settle out of court. They were more concerned with restraining their neighbours' conflicts than with enforcing impersonal regulations. Their task was to restore personal relationships, rather than to secure convictions. In the mid-eighteenth century, the Wiltshire justice William Hunt found that much of his work in dealing with cases of assault and theft constituted acting as an arbitrator. Appearance in court was a last resort.[1]

Slander was another area where Justices intervened. In Boldon (Durham), Edmund Tew dealt with several rumours of sexual infidelity, and with a woman upset at being accused of witchcraft.[2] Such arbitration was in gradual decline by c.1800. Parish notables ceased to seek judicial mediation, and rural Justices withdrew from close involvement in the lives of those they governed.[3]

RIOT

Keeping the peace was an important role for the individual Justice. If serious disturbances broke out, it was his personal responsibility to take action. From 1714, he was authorised to read the Riot Act and to call for troops to put down rioting. Rioting was not always easy to deal with. In 1586, a barge carrying food was stopped on the Severn by a crowd of 500 to 600 people. Justices who read the Riot Act failed to disperse them, and the Sheriff's attempt to arrest the ringleaders failed. Two weeks later another barge was stopped.[4]

ADMINISTRATION OF JUSTICE

Individual Justices dealt with criminal activities ranging from the pettiest misdemeanour to serious offences such as rick-burning, poaching and murder. However, until the eighteenth century they could only exercise summary jurisdiction over misdemeanours, such as vagabondage; everything else went to Quarter Sessions and perhaps from thence to Assizes. In 1663, only some seventy offences were subject to the Justices' summary jurisdiction; by 1776, the number was over 200. The right to trial by jury was gradually abrogated as summary jurisdiction was extended. Game offences previously indictable at Quarter Sessions were increasingly tried summarily, without a jury. When, in 1855,

Justices were given summary powers against industrial theft, prosecutions in the Black Country increased dramatically. Prosecutors expected sympathetic hearings before magistrates who were fellow employers. Juries were much less willing to convict.[5]

In civil matters, Justices had wide supervisory powers over vestries and parish officers, with the final say in the appointment of most parish officers (apart from the churchwarden). They oversaw the operation of the Poor Law (see Chapter 8), and allowed accounts. Between 1653 and 1660, they also conducted marriages; no less than 584 were conducted by the Justices of Leeds (Yorkshire).[6] Individual justices signed certificates of burial in woollen, issued passes for vagrants, permitted labourers to go into other counties in search of harvest work (they needed a settlement certificate), licensed the sick to go to Bath or Buxton for their cure, and took the oaths of postal workers not to open the mail in their care. Quarter Sessions frequently delegated matters such as bridge repairs and the oversight of gaols to individual Justices. In the eighteenth century, Parliament transferred some responsibilities, such as the inspection of weights and measures, and the diversion or closing of footpaths, from Quarter Sessions to individual Justices.

Justices frequently acted on their own authority, sometimes even without statutory backing. The precise wording of statutes could easily be ignored. Convicts were sent to Houses of Correction when the penalty actually prescribed was the stocks. Vagrants were 'passed' to their place of settlement without a whipping, which was quite illegal. The standard textbook commented that 'Kings have been censured for setting themselves above the law, but Justices of the Peace have been suffered to pass unnoticed'.[7]

Appeals against the judgements of individual justices could be made to Quarter Sessions, or, by writ of *certiorari*, to the central courts. In practice, four-fifths of appeals to Quarter Sessions were by parish officers appealing against removal orders that would cost them money.

Some tasks were exercised in pairs. Settlement examinations, and maintenance orders for bastards, both required two Justices. Roman Catholics wanting to travel also required permission from two Justices. Assaults by servants upon masters, game law infringements and making 'deceitful cloth' were amongst the offences which could be punished by two Justices sitting together. After 1815, roads and footpaths could be closed by any two Justices acting summarily. Liquor licencing and highway maintenance both required special sessions. The rise of Petty Sessions in the eighteenth century gradually decreased the powers which Justices could exercise alone.

CRIMINAL PROCEDURE

When a complaint was made to a Justice of the Peace, he took depositions from the complainant and any witnesses. Apprehension of the offender was up to the victim, although constables could raise the hue and cry if called upon to do so. From the eighteenth century, many rewards for information on crimes were advertised in the newspapers; they can be searched for a fee using the British Newspaper Archive (www.britishnewspaperarchive.co.uk).

Upon arrest, the accused was examined by the Justice. Examinations were important documents in the prosecution of offenders. The Justice's task was more that of a policeman than a judge: he was 'charged to assemble a prosecuting brief that would stiffen and supplement the case presented orally by the victim-prosecutor in court'.[8] He was not expected to look for evidence in favour of the defendant. The accused was normally examined first to see if he would confess; then witnesses were asked to comment on the prisoner's examination. Inadequate examinations by Justices frequently frustrated trials at both Quarter Sessions and Assizes.

The best opportunity for the accused to defend himself was the initial examination. It was then that he had 'his first and last chance to give a coherent explanation in his defence'.[9] One in six cases of felonious property crimes that came before individual justices were dismissed.[10] Nevertheless, if the Justice was faced with a sworn accusation by a victim who was prepared to prosecute, he had to either bail the accused or commit him for trial. As late as 1746, Michael Dalton argued that 'even though it shall appear to the Justice that the prisoner is not guilty' his best course was to commit him.[11] That must partly explain why Grand Juries subsequently threw out many indictments.

In the eighteenth century, the role of the examining Justice gradually changed. Increasingly, Justices conducted their examinations in public, enabling defence lawyers to be present. They, of course, endeavoured to prevent their clients incriminating themselves – which was the point of the examination. By the end of the century, defendants could cross-examine witnesses. The Indictable Offences Act of 1848, finally established the principle that the magistrate's examination was to be a judicial inquiry, in which the defendant might be discharged, rather than a gathering of evidence for the prosecution.[12] The collection of evidence became the responsibility of the new police forces. Following examination, Justices could either commit defendants to prison, or grant them bail. Bail was granted by recognizance.

RECOGNIZANCES

The recognizance[13] is perhaps the commonest type of document emanating from individual Justices. It is a bond whereby the person bound undertakes to perform a specific action or pay a monetary penalty to the Crown. Two sureties stood bound with the principal. If the condition was fulfilled, the recognizance became void. The names, abodes and occupations of those bound are given, together with the name(s) of the Justice(s) involved. Recognizances are therefore useful sources for tracing individuals, for assessing the extent to which Justices of the Peace were assiduous in their duties, and for researching the occupations prevalent in particular places.

Recognizances frequently required the persons bound to appear at the next Quarter Sessions, or perhaps the Assizes, in order to answer charges. Recognizances in these cases served as bail, and were useful means of controlling suspected or accused persons without committing them to the county gaol. They could not, incidentally, be confined anywhere else.

There were other uses too. Quarrelling neighbours might be bound to keep the peace towards each other. Victims of crime were bound in order to ensure that they undertook prosecutions. Witnesses might also be bound to appear. The fathers of bastards had to enter bonds to pay maintenance. Alehouse keepers, badgers (itinerant pedlars) and others, had to enter into recognizances to keep the conditions of their licences. Officers, such as High Constables, had to enter into bonds for the proper conduct of their duties; those liable to be summoned to musters sometimes had to give security for their appearance. Recognizances could be used to control bad behaviour, such as drunkenness or defamation; offenders could be bound over to be of good behaviour. Barrators – those who stirred up quarrels and strife – could be bound over to keep the peace; if a Justice was subsequently able to reconcile the parties, the recognizance might be marked *concordantur* – 'they are agreed'.

Occasionally, recognizances provide useful information on the reasons for binding. Those taken by Sir Timothy Lowe of Bromley (Kent) frequently give very full explanations of the circumstances at issue, and describe the characters of those bound. For example, two men accused of excessive wife-beating were bound over to stop doing so; each was instructed to 'well and honestly order and govern his said wife and not otherwise chastise and correct her than lawfully and reasonably'. Sir Timothy's early seventeenth-century recognizances were apt to describe men in terms such as 'a person of disorderly behaviour, a fighter, a frequenter of alehouses, a player of unlawful games', or 'a person of evil demeanour, a common quarreler, a common drunkard, a common slanderer of honest persons and one that maketh debate betwixt man and wife and an accustomed rayler against the King's Majesty's honest subjects'.[14]

Recognizances may be found amongst Quarter Sessions records. Some were endorsed with a discharge, indicating that the matter had been settled without recourse to Quarter Sessions. Sometimes, a more formal release from the recognizance was drawn up. Many led to no further action. Clerks of the Peace kept registers of recognizances.

WARRANTS

Warrants were the means by which Justices of the Peace, both individually and collectively, issued their orders, for example to search for stolen goods or to require the appearance of a suspected felon before them. Warrants could be directed to a variety of officers: the Sheriff, the bailiff, the constable or even private individuals. Unfortunately, not many survive; copies were rarely kept. They did, however, lead to suspects appearing before Quarter Sessions, and to the preparation of innumerable recognizances.

JUSTICING BOOKS

Much of the out-of-Sessions activities of Justices went unrecorded. However, handbooks for Justices usually recommended that they keep records of the cases which came before them. Many 'Justicing Books' survive; there are at least ten for Kent alone.[15] They were private documents, so are most likely to be found amongst family papers. They reveal the great variety of matters that came before individual Justices. The Justicing Book of Sir Richard Colt Hoare of Stourton (Wiltshire) records, on its first page, that in the summer of 1785 he dealt with a case of assault, a complaint 'against Samuel Read for having run away from his service', and the mother of an illegitimate child who had to swear to its paternity.[16] Sir Richard Wyatt's deposition book is entirely devoted to examinations, informations and depositions.[17] Thomas Dixon did not attend Quarter Sessions between 1791 and 1798, but his Justicing Book shows he was a moderately busy Justice 'in my house at Riby'.[18]

Sir Richard Colt Hoare, Justice of the Peace. Frontispiece to his History of Modern Wiltshire.

The wide area over which a Justice of the Peace could exercise his authority is illustrated by the Justicing Book of Edward Tew, the rector of Boldon (Durham); cases came to him from an area extending from South Shields almost to Durham. Tew dealt with many coastal traders. He removed one pauper as far as Dartmouth (Devon), although whether he actually arrived at his destination is not known.[19] Many entries concern the failure of employers to pay their servants, or to provide them with sufficient food. Tew also recorded many letters written to overseers and employers; one wonders whether his letter-writing was typical of other justices.

JUSTICES' LETTERS

Many letters from Justices can be found amongst Quarter Sessions records. They cover a wide range of subjects – purveyance, poor relief, and crime amongst them. In 1608, William Ingram sent his apologies for absence from Worcestershire Sessions to the Clerk of the Peace; in 1613, there was a letter complaining that there were too many inns around Droitwich whose publicans did not attend church.[20]

FURTHER READING

The activities of justices out of sessions are discussed in:
- Oberwiteler, P. 'Crime and authority in eighteenth century England: law enforcement on the local level', *Historical Social Research* 15(2), 1990, pp.3–34.

Much can be learnt from the notebooks of individual justices, which recorded their deliberations in and out of sessions. A number of these have been published, as have various official papers collected by Justices. Those used here include:

Durham
- Morgan, Gwenda, & Rushton, Peter, eds. *The Justicing Notebook (1750-64) of Edmund Tew, Rector of Boldon.* (Surtees Society 205, 2000).

Middlesex
- Paley, R. ed. *Justice in Eighteenth Century Hackney: the Justicing Notebook of Henry Norris and the Hackney Petty Sessions Book.* (London Record Society Publications 28, 1991).

Norfolk
- Saunders, H.W., ed. *The Official Papers of Sir Nathaniel Bacon of Stiffkey, Norfolk, as Justice of the Peace, 1580-1620.* (Camden 3rd series 26, Royal Historical Society, 1915).
- Brook, F.W., ed. 'Supplementary Stiffkey papers', *Camden Miscellany 15.* (Camden 3rd series 52, Royal Historical Society, 1936).
- Rosenheim, James M., ed. *The Notebook of Robert Doughty, 1662-1665.* (Norfolk Record Society 54, 1989).

Surrey
- Silverthorne, Elizabeth, ed. *The Deposition Book of Richard Wyatt, J.P., 1767-1776.* (Surrey Record Society 30, 1978).

Wiltshire
- Crittall, Elizabeth, ed. *The Justicing Notebook of William Hunt, 1744-1749.* (Wiltshire Record Society 37, 1982).

Chapter 5

QUARTER SESSIONS

Justices of the Peace met together regularly at Quarter Sessions, four times each year, in the weeks after Epiphany, Easter, Midsummer and Michaelmas.[1] Some Benches met regularly in the same county town; others itinerated. A few held separate Sessions for different parts of their county; for example, the Sessions for West Kent was held at Maidstone, for East Kent at Canterbury. There were separate Commissions for the Yorkshire Ridings, and for the Parts of Lincolnshire.

Some towns had separate Quarter Sessions. Exeter, Bristol and London were counties in their own right. Many smaller boroughs, such as Great Torrington (Devon), and Guildford (Surrey), also held their own Quarter Sessions, outside of the jurisdiction of the county Bench. Haverfordwest (Pembrokeshire) even had its own Lord Lieutenant. The activities of borough Quarter Sessions are not within the scope of this book.

Quarter Sessions presided over counties, varying in size from Rutland, of 147 square miles, to Devon, 2,590 square miles. Many had detached portions; for example, Furness lay in Lancashire, although bounded by the sea and by Westmorland. County boundaries were amongst the most enduring features of English local government.

The tasks dealt with by Quarter Sessions were many and varied. The growth in its powers were outlined in Chapter 3. It exercised judicial, executive, and even some legislative powers: Justices had no concept of the separation of powers. However, the court only acted on judicial process, even for administrative purposes: there had to be presentment and indictment before money could be spent on bridges. Occasionally, Quarter Session orders amounted to legislation. They could prohibit the keeping of fairs and revels, disqualify publicans from serving as constables, restrict the issue of badgers' licences, adapt the

Exeter Castle. Quarter Sessions and Assizes were held here, and prisoners were incarcerated.

Poor Law as they saw fit (as the Berkshire magistrates notoriously did at Speenhamland), or even ban paupers from keeping dogs.

Despite these powers, the Bench was frequently ineffective. In 1387, Oxfordshire Justices attempted to secure the appearance of twenty-six felons; only six were actually tried and convicted.[2] In 1596, it was estimated that only one felon in five was successfully brought to book.[3] In the mid-eighteenth century, Sir John Fielding argued that 'not one in a Hundred of these robbers are taken in the fact'.[4]

It did not help that the concept of order held by the gentry was not always accepted by the lower orders. Quarter Sessions orders prohibiting wakes and revels were frequently issued, but almost as frequently ignored. The West Riding Justices' attempt to ban cock-fighting in the 1650s predictably failed.[5] The tithingman sent to disperse a banned revel at Langford Budville (Somerset) in 1656 was attacked by men engaged in cudgelling.[6]

The authorities could be even more ineffective when more substantial issues were at stake. When the Crown wished to disafforest royal hunting parks such as Selwood (Wiltshire) and Gillingham (Dorset), neither Justices of the Peace, Sheriffs nor even Deputy Lieutenants, could control the opposition of aggrieved tenants and poor cottagers.

During the Civil War, Sessions sometimes could not even be held. In Wiltshire, the Justices did not meet for two years after the Trinity 1644 Sessions.[7] When meetings resumed, they had to deal with offices vacant, funds misappropriated, taxes unpaid, records lost, routine interrupted, vagrants unrestrained, the poor unrelieved, bridges damaged and roads neglected. The records reflect Parliament's victory. Where pre-war records referred to 'Jurors for the Lord the King', Interregnum records referred to 'Jurors for the Keepers of the Liberties of England', and, subsequently, 'Jurors for the Lord Protector of the Commonwealth'. Even more noticeable was the substitution of English for Latin. During and after the war, security was a prominent issue. Interregnum Justices watched the movements of Royalists closely. After the Restoration, the activities of former Parliamentarians demanded equally close attention. Justices undertook searches for arms, and interrogated anyone suspected of plotting for the wrong side.

Sessions were summoned by a precept addressed to the Sheriff from two Justices of the Peace, or from the Clerk of the Peace, notifying him of the date and place of meeting. The Sheriff proclaimed the Sessions, summoning High Constables, those wishing to make complaints and jurors for both the grand and petty juries. He attended himself, with his under-Sheriffs and bailiffs. Hundred Bailiffs summoned sufficient men to form local juries of inquiry. Jury panels in late sixteenth century Staffordshire could number as many as 100, although numbers were declining.[8]

JURIES

The statutory qualification for jury service from 1595 was ownership of lands valued at 80s per annum. This was increased to £10 in 1692. From 1601, Sheriffs were supposed to compile full listings of qualified freeholders; in 1606, responsibility for this task was transferred to Justices of the Peace. Two copies were produced, one for the Sheriff, the other for the Clerk of Assize. From 1696, constables prepared lists of those qualified to serve for the Michaelmas Quarter Sessions; these were copied by Clerks of the Peace into special freeholders' books. Another book was required by an Act of 1730; Sheriffs had to record the services of each man, and post lists of those eligible for service in parish churches. The County Juries Act of 1825 altered procedures: the lists had to be compiled by constables and churchwardens, delivered to Petty Sessions each September, and taken to Michaelmas Quarter Sessions by High Constables. The Clerk of the Peace used these lists to compile duplicate freeholders' books, one of which he kept; the other was passed to the Sheriff for use as the Jurors' book for the forthcoming year.

Under the Tudors and Stuarts, finding sufficient jurors was difficult. Nevertheless, the composition of Grand Juries was carefully controlled, indicating the importance attached to their functions. In the eighteenth century, recruitment became easier: service conferred social status. Jury lists and freeholders' books provide comprehensive annual directories of gentry, substantial yeomen and prosperous tradesmen.[9] In more recent centuries, many were printed, sometimes giving addresses and occupations as well as names.

A number of different juries had to be summoned. The Grand Jury was chosen from 'the most sufficient freeholders', and frequently consisted of High Constables. Jurors served repeatedly (at least in Cheshire), and were considered to be 'better acquainted with the common grievance of the Countrie, then Justices are'.[10] They determined

Freeholders liable to serve as Jurymen, from a Wiltshire Freeholders Book. (Wiltshire & Swindon History Centre A1/265/8.)

whether indictments were 'true bills' to be tried before the Justices. Their own presentments gradually ceased to have much to do with criminal matters, concentrating on such matters as bad roads, collapsed bridges, disorderly alehouses, excessive vagrancy and corrupt or inefficient officials. They petitioned the Crown on such matters as Ship Money and (in 1642) the control of the Militia. In the eighteenth and nineteenth centuries, they were increasingly consulted before new legislation was considered by Parliament. The Grand Jury acted as the voice of the county, although it had its most decisive role at Assizes (see Chapter 12).

Juries of Hundreds and liberties had tasks similar to those of the Grand Jury, for their area. In 1719 Essex jurors were instructed to present the state of roads and bridges, the abuses of alehouse keepers, and the depredations of poachers.[11] Hundred juries gradually became obsolete, their role in presentment taken over by constables. In Wiltshire, they ceased to be empanelled in 1782.[12] Petty juries, consisting of twelve men, heard the actual trials of criminal cases and pronounced verdicts. The distinction between grand and petty juries was not always clear; in late sixteenth-century Staffordshire both seem to have acted as the jury of accusation.[13]

PROCEDURE

Quarter Sessions procedures evolved over the centuries. For example, presentments and indictments were originally identical, and differentiation between them took centuries to develop. The Grand Jury emerged by the seventeenth century from a variety of juries of inquiry. There was 'little method or arrangement of business'[14] until the eighteenth century, when concern to enhance the 'majesty' of proceedings, combining with the need for greater efficiency, led to the rationalisation of procedures. Only a rough guide to what actually took place can be given here.[15]

Sessions began with a sermon. The Justices were then escorted to the court by the Under-Sheriff and bailiffs. The Crier proclaimed the Sessions, the Clerk of the Peace read the Commission, and the Sheriff returned his precept, with the *nomina ministrorum*.[16] The crier called over the names of those required to be present, recording absences. Reasons for absence, such as illness or death, were noted, as were fines imposed on defaulters. Even absent Justices could be fined. Fines were recorded in estreats.

Justices of the Peace then put in their examinations, with their recognizances requiring the appearance of defendants in court. Coroners handed in their inquests and Hundred Bailiffs handed their lists of potential jurymen to the Sheriff. He selected the petty juries, subject to Justices' approval. If insufficient jurors appeared, freeholders present in court could be called. Juries were sworn, and the charge was delivered.

A nineteenth-century jury.

The charge instructed the Grand Jury – and sometimes inexperienced Justices – in their duties. In 1580, the Wiltshire jurors were told that they were to inquire into three matters: whether 'God be truely honoured', whether 'Her Majestie was truly obeyed', and whether 'Her Majesties subjects be in peace'.[17] After the Restoration, Sir Peter Leicester's charges provided 'essentially elegant homilies on the nature of English law', directed at the many young and inexperienced Justices who sat on the post-Restoration Bench.[18] Charges could be heavily political. In the 1640s, many justified taking up arms against the Crown. The Restoration saw many lectures on the iniquities of republicanism. In the early 1700s, charges frequently debated the validity of Tory and

Whig principles. A century later, they sometimes argued the case for reform.

The charge was the responsibility of the chairman, who acted as the deputy of the *Custos Rotulorum*. Frequently, the most senior Justice present served. In addition to presenting the charge, the chairman kept order during proceedings, ruled on points of law and pronounced sentence. He was, however, merely *primus inter pares* amongst the Bench. By the early eighteenth century, chairmen were being elected; the West Riding Quarter Sessions resolved to elect one in 1709.[19] Increasingly, the chairmanship was held for longer periods than just a single session, allowing chairmen to exercise supervision between sessions. In the nineteenth century, separate chairmen for civil and criminal matters began to be appointed.

During the reading of the charge, the Clerk of the Peace wrote out the names of the several juries, for the information of jury foremen. The court then received sacrament certificates, oaths of allegiance and declarations against transubstantiation. The crier then called for indictments from prosecutors, and the Grand Jury withdrew to consider them, together with the presentments, informations and petitions it had received. In the thirteenth century, presentment and indictment were interchangeable terms. However, by the sixteenth century, the two terms referred to documents which could be quite different.

Indictments were written on parchment (in Latin until 1733), and were usually based on gaol calendars. In Caernarvonshire, they commenced '*Inquiratur pro domino rege si . . .*': 'Let inquiry be made for the Lord the King . . .'.[20] They gave the name, parish and occupation of the accused, the year, date and place of the offence, the name of the victim if appropriate, the value of any goods stolen, and the supposed intention of the accused. They might be endorsed with further information as cases proceeded. The foreman of the Grand Jury endorsed them as either *billa vera* (a true bill), or *ignoramus*, which ended the matter (unless further evidence subsequently appeared). Indictments merely provided a statement of prosecution cases, based upon Justices' preliminary examinations, so it is not surprising that *ignoramus* verdicts were frequent. Magistrates' examinations developed a more thoroughly judicial character in the late eighteenth and nineteenth centuries, and consequently Grand Jury deliberations gradually lost their purpose. That process continued as the police took over the task of prosecution. The Grand Jury was moribund for almost a century, and finally abolished in 1948.

The court also proceeded by means of presentment. Presentments, like indictments, were endorsed *billa vera* or *ignoramus*, and sometimes initiated criminal prosecutions. Many concerned administrative matters. They could be made by High Constables, Hundred juries, the Grand Jury and individual Justices. Sometimes, constables and jurors subscribed the same presentment. High Constables made presentments on the state of their Hundreds, reporting such matters as recusants, the keeping of disorderly houses, and the harbouring of vagrants. They also passed on the presentments of parish constables. These were frequently responses to questionnaires issued by Assize judges, and included many matters not likely to be prosecuted by private individuals. A reconstructed questionnaire from Worcestershire is in the box below. The resultant presentments provided much useful information for Quarter Sessions to proceed upon, and also for researchers to analyse.

Questions probably posed to
Worcestershire Constables, c.1635

1. What taverners, vintners selling wine, and cooks are there in the parish?
2. At what rate do bakers sell bread?
3. Who keeps ordinaries or victualing tables in their houses?
4. What rates are charged at inns for men and for servants?
5. Are any unlawful games practised in taverns or victualing houses?
6. What price is charged by innkeepers for horses and their food?
7. Who sell ale; are they licensed or unlicensed?
8. Is any tobacco grown?
9. Do any lodge rogues, vagabonds, or suspected persons?
10. Are watch and ward duly kept: are rogues found wandering?
11. Are the highways and bridges in good repair?
12. Are there any recusants, seminaries or Jesuits in the parish?
13. Are there any inordinate tipplers or drunkards, common swearers, or other idle and disorderly persons in the parish?

High constables could present parish constables who defaulted on their obligations. In the eighteenth century, however, there was an increasing tendency for constables to neglect presentments and to simply report *omne bene* – all well. The practice of presentment by High Constables and Hundred juries gradually became moribund, and was abolished in 1827.

Grand Jury presentments frequently concerned more general matters. In late-Elizabethan Norfolk, they probably played an important role in attacking patentees.[21] At the outbreak of the Civil War, Grand Juries helped to determine which side the county supported. In 1640, the Worcestershire Grand Jury petitioned Parliament against the powers of the Council of Wales and the Marches.[22] More routinely, the Wiltshire Grand Jury in 1677 requested the Bench to order that a certificate of conformity be produced before alehouse licences, were granted.[23] In 1679, Charles II sought the support of Grand Juries for his actions during the Exclusion crisis. Eighteenth-century Grand Juries were frequently packed by the Sheriff with his supporters, and used for party political purposes.

Presentments made by Justices of the Peace usually concerned some public nuisance. The state of the roads attracted increasing attention in the eighteenth century. So did bridges, gaols and parish workhouses. By the early nineteenth century, Justice's presentments had become a standard method of initiating administrative action: Clerks of the Peace made out presentments, seeking Justices prepared to sign them and implement action.

Whilst the Grand Jury was deliberating, the Justices spent time dealing with routine administration. Statutes were proclaimed; statutory appointments were made; county rates, wages, and the prices of ale and soap were fixed. Then, dinner was served.

After dinner, trials commenced. Many accused were bailed rather than gaoled before trial. Those who failed to appear were summoned by 'process'. Failure to answer a writ of *venire facias* could lead to various further writs, and culminate in an *exigi facias*, or writ of outlawry. The outlaw could be killed on sight, and have all their goods seized. Despite these provisions, however, attendance in court was difficult to enforce. In seventeenth-century Surrey, hundreds of writs were issued to compel attendance; the same names appeared repeatedly.[24]

The gaoler brought in his prisoners, and trials on indictments marked *billa vera* proceeded, or were referred to Assizes. Pleas might be noted on indictments: *cogn* (*cognovit*) for a guilty plea, or *po se* (*ponet* se) if the accused asked to be tried by jury. If he refused to plea, *stat mute* or *nichil dicit* was noted. Occasionally, cases were postponed, and the prisoner returned to gaol until the next Sessions. If the indictment was endorsed *ignoramus*, or a prosecutor failed to appear, the accused would be discharged at the end of the Session.

It was up to victims to lay information before a Justice, to gather evidence, to make sure that witnesses attended, and to prosecute. Examining magistrates did not necessarily attend court, although they did send in their examinations. Many victims were, unsurprisingly, unwilling to prosecute, especially as they had to pay their own costs.[25] Many cases went unreported or unsolved; in 1596, it was suggested that perhaps 80 per cent of offenders escaped justice.[26]

Victims' reluctance to prosecute increasingly led the authorities to offer rewards for the successful apprehension and prosecution of felons. An Act of 1692 offered a £40 reward for the apprehension and conviction of highwaymen; the 'Tyburn ticket', created under an Act of 1699, offered exemption from parish office to all those who successfully prosecuted a felon. From 1752, judges could order costs to be paid to successful prosecutors. Subsequent legislation, culminating in the Criminal Justice Act of 1826, provided expenses to witnesses as well as prosecutors. In 1785, the Surrey Bench initiated a fund to reward successful prosecutions of felons.[27] In the eighteenth century, a steadily increasing number of associations for the prosecution of criminals were founded. These were mutual aid societies which enabled many to initiate prosecutions who would not otherwise have done so. From 1818, costs were met by the county, and from c.1850, the new police forces increasingly took over the task of prosecution.

The court heard a number of cases – perhaps as many as a dozen – at the same time. Once sufficient prisoners had been arraigned, the Sheriff returned a petty jury, the cases were heard, and juries delivered their verdicts, which required unanimity from the fifteenth century onwards. Each case took only a few minutes; juries frequently did not leave the courtroom to deliberate. Defence lawyers were not permitted. It was not until the early eighteenth century that cases began to be considered separately, and not until the nineteenth century that the confrontation between accuser and accused became a confrontation between prosecuting lawyer and defence lawyer.

Trials were followed by the hearing of traverses. These were defences against accusations of misdemeanours (see below) which had been adjourned from the previous Sessions to allow defendants to prepare their traverse, that is, their defence. Many concerned administrative matters such as liability for bridge repairs. Each case required a separate jury, and both sides could retain attorneys. Judgement frequently turned on complex issues of ancient rights and liberties.

Traverses were followed by the hearing of grievances, before the Grand Jury was discharged. Verdicts in criminal cases were then returned. For guilty verdicts, *cul.* (*culpabilis*) was written on the indictment; if not guilty, *non cul.* Goods of felons could be seized, so juries were asked whether there were any; *cat. null.* (*catalla nulla* – no goods) was the usual response. The final question was whether the accused had fled; the answer was usually no, so *nec retraxit* was written.

Recognizances were then called over, the oldest first, and either discharged or continued. Anyone who had not appeared on a recognizance without good reason could be estreated. Bastardy and settlement cases were then heard, alehouse and badgers' licences were granted, and general orders made. Sentencing then took place, and the Session came to an end. There was no appeal against most convictions and sentences at Quarter Sessions until 1907.

CRIMES AND MISDEMEANOURS

Common crimes in the early modern period included larceny, assault, riot, fraud and embezzlement. Quarter Sessions rarely tried anything more serious than petty larceny (that is, theft of goods valued at under 12d), frequently committed by vagrants and 'wandering persons'. The details of goods stolen provide a useful insight into the nature of articles in daily use, and may usefully be compared with probate inventories. The places from which they were stolen are also interesting: sheep rustling from the village common was easy, burglary of a dwelling house more difficult.

Until the late eighteenth century, assault was frequently regarded as a matter for arbitration; Justices acknowledged agreement between the parties by imposing small fines. More serious cases, such as homicide, robbery with violence and burglary, were usually reserved for the Assizes. Two Marian statutes required Justices to certify examinations and informations of felons to Assizes. From 1590, Commissions exhorted the Justices to refer all *casus difficultatis* (difficult cases) to Assize judges. Cases could also be removed by writ of *certiorari* to a superior court, placing pressure on prosecutors to settle before costs mounted.

Quarter Sessions also dealt with misdemeanours, that is, offences against economic and social regulations. Failure to assist in communal tasks, such as refusal to serve as a parish officer, to perform statutory labour on the highways or to pay rates, might result in indictment. Those who blocked the highways with muck heaps, hedges, ditches and sheep folds, grew tobacco, or begged without a licence might appear. Unlicensed and disorderly alehouse keepers and their customers occupied much of the time of the Bench, which also kept an eye on their prices. There were no less than 480 presentments for alehouse offences at the Michaelmas sessions, 1619 in the North Riding of Yorkshire.[28]

Poaching and related offences, such as deer stealing and keeping game dogs, were common offences, since they offered poor men the opportunity to provide for their tables. Vagrancy was also an offence (see Chapter 8), but perhaps more frequently dealt with by parish constables and local Justices than by Quarter Sessions.

Trading offences, such as engrossing (unfairly buying up all the goods in the market and reselling them at a higher price), or conducting a trade without undergoing an apprenticeship, were frequent subjects of complaints under the Tudors and Stuarts. Disputes between apprentices and masters were common. Apprentices might be idle, dishonest, or abscond. Masters might inflict immoderate 'correction' or fail to provide for apprentices properly. Justices could cancel indentures or re-assign apprentices to new masters. Pauper apprentices are discussed in Chapter 8. Other relationships between masters and servants also came under scrutiny. Servants are discussed in Chapter 7, wages in Chapter 10.

Rioting could be a serious matter: in Oxford, racist riots against Welsh students in 1389 led to four deaths.[29] Legally, a riot was anything done in a violent and tumultuous manner. Many were attempts to rescue persons under arrest. Others were protests against unemployment and famine. Many offences in Caernarvonshire probably stemmed from disputes over ownership of land.[30]

Attendance at church was expected by the community and enforced by law (see Chapter 9). The Puritans directed their ire at 'profane swearers', at alehouse keepers who sold drink at the time of divine service, at carriers who travelled on Sundays, at those who played 'unlawful games' and at anyone carrying on their trade on the Sabbath. Such offences could result in appearance before the Bench, although they were frequently dealt with by a single Justice or in ecclesiastical courts.

SENTENCING

The punishment for felony was death. The number of crimes liable to capital punishment increased from fifty in 1603 to over 200 by the early nineteenth century. The law, however, was intended to deter criminals, rather than to punish them – only a few instances of severity were needed to achieve deterrence. In practice, courts frequently mitigated penalties by reducing the seriousness of charges, or by recommending pardons. The accused could sometimes plead 'clergy', claiming that his ability to read proved his entitlement to trial in an ecclesiastical court – which could not impose the death penalty. Clergied offenders did, however, suffer branding. Benefit of clergy will be considered in more detail in Chapter 12.

Branding, whipping, the pillory and hanging were standard punishments until the late eighteenth century. Minor offences might be punished by fines. The Bench took into account the fact that many convicts had been imprisoned before their trial, so had already been punished. Crimes thought to merit the death penalty were generally sent to Assizes.

In the early eighteenth century, the introduction of transportation caused major changes in sentencing practice. For the ensuing century or so, transportation to America, and subsequently to Australia, became a frequent sentence, and executions were drastically reduced. Sentences of imprisonment also replaced them. By c.1830, executions had ceased to be regular events, despite the number of capital offences still on the statute book.

Increasing public revulsion against violence was also demonstrated by the ending of public punishment for female offenders. But the same revulsion also led Justices to treat assault with much greater seriousness. The old practice of informal arbitration was abandoned. Similarly, juvenile offenders ceased to be treated with leniency.

Sentencing was also affected by considerations of cost. An execution

Iames Nailor Quaker set 2 howers on the Pillory at Westminster whiped by the Hangman to the old Exchainge London, Som dayes after, Stood too howers more on the Pillory at the Exchainge and there had his Tongue Bored throug with a hot Iron, & Stigmatized in the forehead with the Letter B: Decem: 17: anno Dom: 1656:

James Naylor created uproar during the Interregnum when he re-enacted Christ's entry into Jerusalem. He was whipped at the cart's tail, stood in the pillory, and had his tongue bored through.

could cost the county as much as £10 in fees. The cost of transportation averaged five guineas. Whipping and the stocks were much cheaper, and a fine produced income. Such considerations were not unimportant.

JUSTICES AND THE LAW

Justices had a major influence on the development of English law. The confused state of statute law, the wide powers which Justices exercised over the lower classes, and limited supervision, gave Justices the opportunity to shape the law, and in some cases to drive reform. For example, vagrancy offered much scope for Justices of the Peace to ignore the formal law (see Chapter 8). Prison reform originated in the counties.

Local Acts of Parliament, probably mostly influenced by Justices, far outnumbered public general Acts.

If the law became inconvenient, justices circumvented or ignored it. Late fifteenth-century Justices profited from enclosure, and ignored legislation against it. Settlement examinations (see Chapter 8) were frequently taken by a single Justice, although legally two had to be present. When the practice of imprisoning suspects before examination was ruled illegal in 1785, many Justices simply ignored the ruling, despite the potential for heavy damages.[31] If Justices or juries thought that a penalty was too harsh, or were unhappy with a ruling from the central courts, they simply refused to convict. Gleaners (who collected leftover crops from farmers' fields) knew that juries were unlikely to convict them of theft, despite Lord Loughborough's 1788 ruling that gleaning was illegal. The letter of the law, and its practice, were sometimes two entirely different things.[32]

The early nineteenth century saw a number of procedural changes, introduced piecemeal, but dramatically altering the nature of criminal trials. Rules of evidence became much stricter, trials became more adversarial, and the defence of the accused was professionalised. A series of Acts in 1848–9 established standard court procedures, reduced Justices' scope for manoeuvre, and confirmed the notion that only Parliament had the authority to initiate legal change.

ADMINISTRATIVE ACTION

In addition to criminal and civil cases, Quarter Sessions concerned itself with a wide range of administrative matters. Much time was taken up with Poor Law business. Roads and bridges were also important, as were rates and taxes. A wide range of other matters were dealt with, ranging from the management of county buildings, to the ransom of Turkish captives. In the early seventeenth century, Wiltshire Quarter Sessions were instructed to regulate the textile industry, to investigate complaints concerning the manufacture of saltpetre, and to put a stop to the cultivation of tobacco. They had to supply horses for postmasters, and to arrange the carriage of timber for the Navy.[33] In the West Riding, the Bench took action to prevent the spread of plague in the 1630s and 1640s.[34]

The possibility of famine was never far from the minds of Tudor and Stuart Privy Councillors. They required Justices to prevent hoarding, engrossing, regrating (buying up grain to re-sell it in the same market) and non-essential use of corn. Producers of food were required to send it to market. Only the poor were allowed to make purchases during the first hour of a market. The Book of Orders issued in 1630 systematized Justices' duties in these areas, aiming to moderate the symptoms of poverty before economic crises occurred. It insisted that Justices should regularly and systematically carry out their duties, and ensured they did so by instituting a reporting system which provided central government with regular reports from the Justices, via the Assize judges.[35] Charles I made the most systematic attempt to ensure good local government before the nineteenth century. In the long run, he failed. After 1660, for 150 years, central government rarely interfered with Quarter Sessions in purely local matters.

Henceforward, Justices drove county policy, although the need for the Grand Jury to approve administrative action meant that it sometimes assumed responsibility itself, or at least acted as a finance committee. A 1739 Act required a presentment from the Grand Jury before money could be spent from county funds. That marked the high point of the Grand Jury's involvement in administration. Subsequently, jurymen who held office for only one session, and who were increasingly unwilling to present anything, could not meet the dramatically increasing need for active administration.

County expenditure increased ten-fold between 1689 and 1835,[36] as the population increased. The cost of maintaining roads, bridges, hospitals, lunatic asylums and gaols grew substantially. The creation of the Wiltshire Police Force in 1839 required a new police rate in 1840, which equalled the old county rate for all other purposes.[37]

Expenses were met by county rates, levied for specific purposes,[38] although sometimes diverted to other purposes. Soldiers had to be paid, county bridges, hospitals, Houses of Correction and gaols had to be maintained; maimed soldiers had to be given pensions; vagrants had to be 'passed' (see Chapter 8); emergencies had to be met. Counties also contributed annually towards the maintenance of prisoners in the Marshalsea and King's Bench.

Levying separate rates for all of these purposes was increasingly seen as inefficient. In the late seventeenth century some Benches experimented with a 'regular, permanent general fund for various county purposes, to make collection and accounting easier'.[39] In 1739,

The Marshalsea Prison, Southwark. From Walford, E. 'Southwark High Street', in Old and New London, *Vol.6. 1878.*

legislation consolidated the various different levies into a single rate. However, another separate rate was imposed by the Mutiny Act of 1809, which required Justices to pay for the provision of horses and oxen, with drivers and carriages, for armed forces marching through their jurisdiction. London Metropolitan Archives hold printed orders for Mutiny Rates c.1832–56. These give details such as average prices of hay and oats, types of carriages, the numbers of oxen or horses and the weight of loads.

Most rates were paid by tenants, although occasionally the burden was shifted onto landlords. Assessment was according to ancient custom, usually based on land, but sometimes on goods, or on cattle. Some were levied across the whole county; others affected perhaps a Hundred, or even a particular parish. When Redditch was visited by plague in 1625, eleven neighbouring parishes were rated to provide support for the sufferers.[40]

Quarter Sessions set rates and notified High Constables, who apportioned the amount between parishes. Parish constables acted as collectors, paying sums collected to county treasurers. In 1844, rate-collecting became the responsibility of Poor Law Guardians. Quarter Sessions and Assize order books record details of the levies made, and perhaps their apportionment between the parishes. Ratepayers' names may be recorded amongst parish records.

Financial administration was primitive until c.1800. Local Justices oversaw specific works, but county expenses were not properly scrutinised. Bills were simply presented to Quarter Sessions, and payment was ordered, or perhaps referred to a couple of Justices. The steadily increasing pressures of administration eventually led, in the 1790s, to the establishment of permanent committees, and the appointment of professional officers.

The earliest committees were the gaol visitors, who, after 1782, made regular reports to Quarter Sessions. By 1834, Gloucestershire had committees for finance, vagrants, bridges, weights and measures, and other matters. All accounts were submitted to the audit committee before being placed before Quarter Sessions.[41] By contrast, Wiltshire only had a finance committee and visitors for the gaol and private lunatic asylums. To these were added committees for the constabulary (1839), visitors to the county asylum (1849), county rates (1870), licensing (1872), county bridges and highways (1876), boundaries (1883) and a joint committee with other counties on the River Avon fisheries (1866).

HUNDRED COURTS AND PETTY SESSIONS

In Chapter 1, we saw that each county had a number of administrative divisions, variously named. These divisions originally had their own courts. These were the 'third kind of sessions', according to Harrison, 'holden by the high constables and bailiffs . . . wherein the weights and measures are perused by the clerk of the market for the county, who sitteth with them. At these meetings also victualers, and in like sort servants, labourers, rogues and runagates, are often reformed for their excesses.'[42] Many Hundreds were private franchises; where this was the case, their courts were conducted by their lords. There were thirty-nine Hundreds in thirteenth-century Wiltshire; only twelve were in the King's hands.[43] Hundred courts were prone to corruption, frequently lacked impartiality, and became increasingly moribund in the early modern period.

As Hundred Courts withered away, Petty Sessions grew.[44] Counties were too large to be effective judicial and administrative units. Divisional meetings of Justices of the Peace were held as early as the fourteenth century. Worcestershire Justices were holding regular 'monthly meetings' under Elizabeth.[45] The Elizabethan Poor Law required Justices to meet annually in each locality to appoint overseers. The 1630–1 Book of Orders required divisional Justices to meet regularly. The Highways Act 1691 established separate highway sessions to appoint parish surveyors and supervise their activities. A Privy Council order of 1706 required the appointment of Justices in particular divisions to act against Roman Catholics.[46] In the early eighteenth century, Kent Quarter Sessions ordered that alehouse licences, parish officers' oaths, the approval of overseers' accounts and the assessment of poor rates should all be matters for Petty Sessions rather than individual Justices. 'Brewster' sessions were held regularly from 1729 to licence alehouses. Eighteenth-century Petty Sessions became 'the prime focus of judicial power', acquiring clerks and doorkeepers.[47] Quarter Sessions ceased to be the administrative body of first instance, but increasingly heard appeals from Petty Sessions, especially in settlement cases.

Firm statutory foundations were not provided for Petty Sessions until the Petty Sessions Act 1849, followed by the Prosecution Expenses Act 1851; the latter provided for the appointment of salaried clerks.

THE RECORDS OF QUARTER SESSIONS

The formal records of Quarter Sessions vary from county to county, but are likely to include order books, sessions rolls, process books and a variety of other documents. The names of a fair proportion of the lower orders, and most of the yeomanry and gentry, are likely to be mentioned in them.

Formal proceedings were recorded in order books or rolls. A number of fourteenth-century rolls were either collected during the itinerations of the Court of King's Bench, or sent to King's Bench or Chancery in response to writs. Some have been published and are listed below. When King's Bench sat locally, Quarter Sessions ceased to operate, and the superior court heard its cases, which therefore had to be enrolled. When King's Bench ceased to itinerate at the beginning of the fifteenth century, rolls were no longer required.

James I probably issued a general direction to commence keeping Quarter Sessions order or act books; many were begun in his reign. They contain formal orders of the court, both judicial and administrative. Some Clerks of the Peace experimented with keeping records before the formal series of order books commenced; in Wiltshire they commenced when the Clerk began keeping a register of badgers, and subsequently used that register as a notebook to record matters needing his attention.

At the end of each Sessions, Clerks prepared process or indictment books, listing indictments and presentments that required Sheriffs to take action. He also drew up the estreats,[48] listing fines payable. Recusant rolls[49] were sent to the Exchequer. Other paperwork, such as precepts, indictments, jury lists, calendars of prisoners, recognizances, presentments, examinations, petitions and reports, were generally gathered together in Sessions 'rolls' or files. The term 'rolls' is slightly misleading; the documents are frequently tied together with string, rather than stitched together and properly rolled up.[50] Sometimes particular types of documents are filed separately. Most were written by Clerks of the Peace, Sheriffs, or Justices' clerks.

Gaol calendars were written by the gaoler; they listed prisoners, offences, committing Justices and the date of committal. Those serving sentences, including any awaiting transportation to America or Australia, might also be listed.[51] Sometimes calendars were annotated with the court's judgement.

Indictments have already been described. However, pre-nineteenth century indictments can be misleading. Their purpose was very specific:

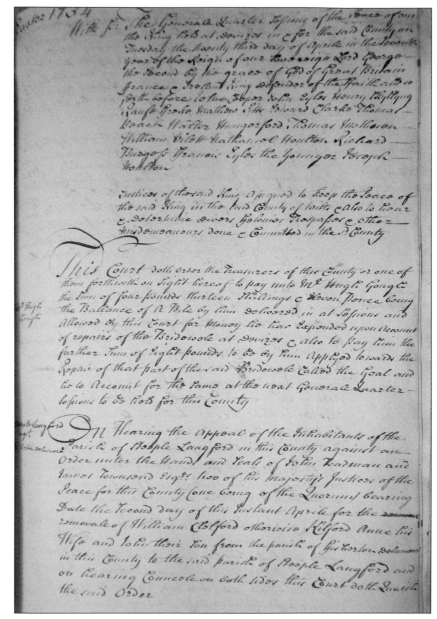

A page from Wiltshire Quarter Sessions Order Book. (Wiltshire & Swindon History Centre A1/160/6.)

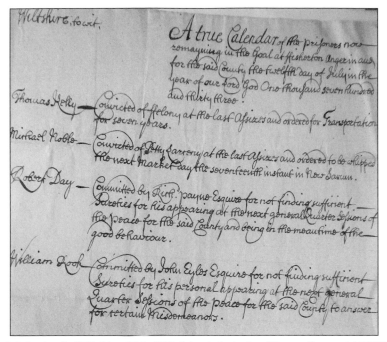

*Gaol Calendar for Wiltshire 1733. (*Wiltshire & Swindon History Centre A1/125/6.)

to ensure that the accused received a proper trial. If they failed to follow the proper form, they could be thrown out for insufficiency. They were therefore worded very precisely, to describe offences against specific statutes, or identify specific common law offences. Accuracy in matters irrelevant to that purpose did not matter. Consequently, what actually happened is not always clear; the status of the accused was usually given as 'labourer' and his stated 'residence' was usually the scene of the crime. Dates on which offences were committed are not to be trusted.

Despite these problems, indictments have been used extensively in studying the history of criminality.[52] Their evidence can be supplemented by examinations, depositions taken before Justices of the Peace, and recognizances (see Chapter 4), frequently filed with them.

A variety of other documents were also filed in sessions rolls. Jury lists are valuable sources of information on the lesser gentry and yeomanry. There are many letters from central government, concerning such matters as harvest failure, forced loans and purveyance. Many petitions were received, perhaps asking the Court for permission to erect cottages, or for a pension for a maimed soldier. They were sometimes annotated to record the court's decision.

Quarter Sessions records can be found in county record offices, which were originally founded to house their records. Much has been lost; the hazards of damp, mice and fire were not easy to guard against. In 1800, the Worcestershire documents 'and particularly the more ancient part of them [were in] an unceiled garret, entirely unarranged and insecure, and the residue irregularly placed in broken and old boxes'.[53] In Cornwall, little survives before the eighteenth century. Pre-nineteenth century Petty Sessions records were particularly susceptible to disappearance: Petty Sessions clerks had no responsibility for keeping them.[54] In Kent, eighteenth-century minute books survive, but generally records only become common after 1879, when clerks were required to deposit registers of convictions, depositions and certificates with Clerks of the Peace.[55]

Calendars of Quarter Sessions records for most counties can now be searched on The National Archives Discovery database http://discovery.nationalarchives.gov.uk; many county record offices also have their own online catalogues. Lancashire order books have been digitised at http://search.ancestry.co.uk/search/db.aspx?dbid=6820.

FURTHER READING
For the criminal jurisdiction of Quarter Sessions and other courts, see:
• Beattie, J.M. *Crime and the Courts in England, 1660-1800*. (Clarendon Press, 1986).

The records of Quarter Sessions are summarily listed by:
• Gibson, Jeremy. *Quarter Sessions Records for Family Historians: a Select List*. (5th ed. Family History Partnership, 2007).

Many editions of Quarter Sessions order books, rolls, and other records are in print. Those with useful introductions used here are listed below. Early rolls for many counties are included in:
• Putnam, Bertha Haven, ed. *Proceedings before the Justices of the Peace in the Fourteenth and Fifteenth centuries, Edward III to Richard III*. (Spottiswoode, Ballantyne & Co., 1938).

Bedfordshire
- 'Sir William Boteler's charges to the Grand Jury at Quarter Sessions, 1643-1647', in Lee, Ross, ed. *Law and Local Society in the Time of Charles I: Bedfordshire and the Civil War.* (Bedfordshire Historical Record Society 65, 1986), pp.57–110.

Cheshire
- Morrill, J.S. *The Cheshire Grand Jury 1625-1659: a Social and Administrative Study.* (Leicester University Dept. of English Local History occasional papers 3rd series 1, Leicester University Press, 1976).

Dorset
- Hearing, Terry, & Bridges, Sarah, eds. *Dorset Quarter Sessions Order Book, 1625-1638: a Calendar.* (Dorset Record Society 14, 2006).

Durham
- Fraser, C.M., ed. *Durham Quarter Sessions Rolls, 1471-1625.* (Surtees Society 198, 1991).

Essex
- Allen, D.H., ed. *Essex Quarter Sessions Order Book, 1652-1661.* (Essex Edited Texts 1. Essex Record Office Publications 65, Essex County Council, 1964).

Gloucestershire
- Kimball, Elisabeth Guernsey, ed. 'Rolls of the Gloucestershire Sessions of the Peace, 1361-1398', *Transactions of the Bristol and Gloucestershire Archaeological Society* 62, 1940, p.112.
- Wyatt, Irene, ed. *Calendar of Summary Convictions at Petty Sessions, 1781-1837.* (Gloucestershire Record Series 22, Bristol & Gloucestershire Archaeological Society, 2008).

Hertfordshire
- Hardy, W.J., et al, eds. *Hertford County Records.* 10 vols. (Hertford: C.E. Longmore, et al, 1905–57).

Kent

- Putnam, Bertha Haven, ed. *Kent Keepers of the Peace, 1316-1317.* (Kent Records. Kent Archaeological Society Records Branch 13, 1933).
- Knafla, Louis A., ed. *Kent at Law 1602: the County Jurisdiction: Assizes and Sessions of the Peace.* (HMSO, 1994).

Lancashire

- Quintrell, B.W., ed. *Proceedings of the Lancashire Justices of the Peace at the Sheriff's Table during Assizes week, 1578-1694.* (Record Society of Lancashire and Cheshire 121, 1981).
- Tait, James, ed. *Lancashire Quarter Sessions Records. Vol.1. Quarter Sessions Rolls, 1590-1606.* (Chetham Society New Series 77, 1917).

Lincolnshire

- Sillem, Rosamund, ed. *Records of Some Sessions of the Peace in Lincolnshire, 1360-1375.* (Lincoln Record Society 30, 1936).
- Kimball, Elisabeth G., ed. *Records of some Sessions of the Peace in Lincolnshire, 1381-1396. Vol.1. The Parts of Kesteven and the Parts of Holland.* (Lincoln Record Society 49, 1955).
- Peyton, S.A., ed. *Minutes of Proceedings in Quarter Sessions held for the Parts of Kesteven in the County of Lincoln, 1674-1695. Part 1.* (Lincoln Record Society 25, 1931).

Middlesex

- Jeaffreson, John Cordy, ed. *Middlesex County Records.* 4 vols. (Middlesex County Records Society, 1886–91). Covers 1550–1688.
- Hardy, W.J., ed. *Calendar of the Sessions Books, 1689 to 1709.* (Sir Richard Nicholson, 1905). Continued to 1752 in typewritten volumes in the British Library.
- Hardy, William Le, ed. *County of Middlesex: Calendar to the Sessions Records. New series.* 4 vols. (Middlesex County Council, 1935–41). Covers 1612 to 1618 in more detail.

Northamptonshire

- Gollancz, Marguerite, ed. *Rolls of the Northamptonshire Sessions of the Peace; roll of the Supervisors, 1314-1316; roll of the Keepers of the Peace 1320.* (Northamptonshire Record Society Publications 11, 1940).

- Wake, Joan, ed. *Quarter Sessions Records of the County of Northampton. Files for 6 Charles I and Commonwealth (A.D. 1630, 1657, 1657-8)*. (Northamptonshire Record Society Publications 1, 1924).

Oxfordshire
- Kimball, Elizabeth G., ed. *Oxfordshire Sessions of the Peace in the Reign of Richard II*. (Oxfordshire Record Society 53, 1983).
- Gretton, Mary Sturge, ed. *Oxfordshire Justices of the Peace in the Seventeenth Century*. (Oxfordshire Record Society 16, 1934).

Shropshire
- Kimball, Elisabeth G., ed. *The Shropshire Peace Roll, 1400-1414*. (Salop County Council, 1959).

Somerset
- Shorrocks, Derek, ed. *Bishop Still's Visitation, 1594, and the 'smale booke' of the Clerk of the Peace for Somerset 1593-5*. (Somerset Record Society 94, 1998).
- Bates, E.H., ed. *Quarter Sessions Records for the County of Somerset*. (Somerset Record Society 23–4, 28, & 34, 1907–19). Covers 1607–77.

Staffordshire
- Burne, S.A.H., et al, eds. *The Staffordshire Quarter Sessions Rolls*. 6 vols. (*Collections for the History of Staffordshire* 3rd series, 1929–49). Covers 1581–1609.

Surrey
- Powell, Dorothy L., & Jenkinson, Hilary, eds. *Surrey Quarter Sessions Records: Order Book and Sessions Rolls, 1659-1661*. (Surrey Record Society 13, 1934). Also published by Surrey County Council. Further vols. cover 1661–3, 1663–6, and 1666–8.

Wiltshire
- Johnson, H.C., ed. *Wiltshire County Records: Minutes of Proceedings in Sessions, 1563 and 1574 to 1592*. (Wiltshire Archaeological and Natural History Society Records Branch 4, 1949).

- Fowle, J.P.M., ed. *Wiltshire Quarter Sessions and Assizes, 1736.* (Wiltshire Archaeological & Natural History Society Records Branch 11, 1955).
- Slocombe, Ivor, ed. *Wiltshire Quarter Sessions Order Book, 1642-1654.* (Wiltshire Record Society 67, 2014).

Yorkshire
- Putnam, Bertha Haven, ed. *Yorkshire Sessions of the Peace, 1361-1364.* (Yorkshire Archaeological Society Record Series 100, 1939).
- Lister, John, ed. *West Riding Sessions Rolls 1597/8-1602.* (Yorkshire Archaeological and Topographical Society Record Series 3, 1888).
- Lister, John, ed. *West Riding Sessions Records, vol.II. Orders 1611-1642; Indictments 1637-1642.* (Yorkshire Archaeological Society Record Series 54, 1915).

Caernarvonshire
- Williams, W. Ogwen, ed. *Calendar of the Caernarvonshire Quarter Sessions Records. Vol.1. 1541-1558.* (Caernarvonshire Historical Society, 1956).

Merionethshire
- Williams-Jones, Keith, ed. *A Calendar of the Merioneth Quarter Sessions rolls. Vol.1. 1733-1765.* (Merioneth County Council, 1965).

Chapter 6

THE CLERK OF THE PEACE AND OTHER OFFICERS

THE CLERK OF THE PEACE

The Clerk of the Peace was the principal administrative officer of Quarter Sessions. His office was first officially mentioned in 1380. Clerks were generally persons of substance, who had perhaps been Sheriffs, coroners or even Members of Parliament. Some early Clerks served in Westminster courts. Occasionally Clerks served two counties simultaneously; Michael Ewen, for example, served both Somerset and Wiltshire from 1770 to 1782.[1] Medieval appointments were sometimes made by the Justices themselves, or sometimes by letters patent (National Archives, series C 66). After 1545, Clerks were appointed by the *Custos Rotulorum* for the life of the *Custos*. From 1688, Quarter Sessions had the power of removal. Clerks' names were enrolled by the Lord Treasurer's Remembrancer from 1717 (National Archives, E 389/407-8). They can also be traced in estreats.

Clerks were required to be 'learned in the law'. Their duties, broadly, included:

- Organising Sessions business and providing legal advice.
- Executing Quarter Sessions' orders.
- Keeping order books and a wide range of other records.
- Liaising with central government.

From 1392, Clerks were paid two shillings for every day spent at sessions; payments are recorded on the pipe rolls. They were entitled to a wide range of fees; almost 100 were enumerated in the *Office of the Clerk of the Peace*, published in 1682. The enrolment of bargains and sales, the taking of recognizances and the registering of badgers'

Robert Incledon, Clerk of the Peace in early eighteenth-century Devon.

licences, all required payment of fees. Fees were regulated by an Act of 1753. Fixed salaries gradually replaced fees in the nineteenth century. Clerks could also practise as attorneys, sometimes on behalf of their own Benches. They frequently held other offices.

Most clerks performed their duties personally. The amount of work involved required most Clerks to employ subordinates. These might include a deputy who could stand in for the Clerk when necessary, attorneys to deal with Justices' correspondence and provide legal advice, and clerks who wrote many of the records we now consult.

Clerks' responsibilities to Quarter Sessions were discussed in Chapter 5. Liaison with central government was also important. Clerks engrossed estreats of fines and amercements for the Exchequer (National Archives, E 372), prepared recusant rolls (National Archives, E 376-7), and promoted county bills in Parliament. For the sixteenth and seventeenth centuries, State Papers in The National Archives contain much information from Clerks. Making returns became a particularly onerous task towards the end of the eighteenth century; many extensive governmental reports are based on evidence provided by Clerks of the Peace. Topics covered included the state of the poor in 1777, charitable donations in 1786 and friendly societies in 1795. During the Napoleonic Wars, Clerks compiled annual reports on Militia officers. In 1801, they organised the first census. The 1831 census was associated with the collection of information on parish registers, which led to a Parliamentary paper on *Parish register abstracts*.[2] These and many similar reports, normally published as Parliamentary papers, provide a huge amount of useful information for local historians.

A detailed study of the Clerk of the Peace, together with a full listing of those who held the office, is provided by:
• Stephens, Edgar, Sir. *The Clerks of the Counties, 1360-1960*. (Society of Clerks of the Peace of Counties and of Clerks of County Councils, 1961).

BRIDGE SURVEYORS
See Chapter 10.

CHIEF CONSTABLES
See Chapter 10.

CUSTOS ROTULORUM
The Commission of the Peace was headed by the *Custos Rotulorum*, or Keeper of the Records. After the Restoration the office was usually held simultaneously with the office of Lord Lieutenant. Technically, the *Custos Rotulorum* was expected to produce whatever records were required at Quarter Sessions and to chair its meetings. In practice, the Clerk of the Peace produced the records, a deputy acted as chairman, and the *Custos* merely acted as a figurehead. His most important functions were to appoint the Clerk of the Peace and to influence appointments to the Bench.

THE CRIER AND THE MARSHALL

Quarter Sessions depended on the work of these minor officials. The Crier made official announcements, called names, and demanded silence in court. The Marshall kept order in court, and escorted the accused. Both officers sometimes undertook other tasks on behalf of Quarter Sessions.

HIGH CONSTABLES

The High Constable was the chief officer of the Hundred, originally appointed by its leet. The appointment was increasingly made by Quarter Sessions. The Constable was expected to be 'of the ablest freeholders, and substantiallest yeomen, next to the degree of gentlemen'.[3] Technically, office was held for one year only. In practice, some held office for life.

Their duties were many and varied. The Statute of Winchester, 1285, required High Constables to view armour twice a year, to present suits of towns and of highways, and to present those who lodged strangers for whom they could not answer. They played important roles in organising musters, impressing soldiers, and checking beacons. For these duties, they were responsible to the Sheriff, and, subsequently, to the Lieutenancy.

High Constables also held Hundred courts, until these gradually withered away in the early modern period. They received parish constables' presentments, and made presentments themselves. They supervised the hiring of servants and executed orders relating to weights and measures. They organised the hue and cry, and watch and ward – the latter primarily to apprehend vagrants, who could be whipped. They were present at both Quarter Sessions and Petty Sessions, and carried out the orders of Justices of the Peace. In Cheshire, they made recommendations to Justices regarding men suitable to be nominated as parish constables.[4] The Justices looked to them to present nuisances such as disordered alehouses and decayed bridges. In 1749–50, the North Riding justices relied on them to put down the cattle plague then raging; they enforced the suspension of markets and fairs for three months.[5] In 1815, Surrey Quarter Sessions required them to undertake regular inspections of public houses.[6] Most importantly, they were responsible for the collection of county rates, purveyance, and other taxes. In many of these duties, High Constables supervised parish constables.

High Constables received minimal remuneration. In the eighteenth century they began to take fees, for example for the inspection of county bridges. They might take 'poundage' on the rates they collected. By the 1830s, many were paid a salary.[7] However, they ceased to collect county rates in 1844, and were abolished in 1869, when the new police forces (see Chapter 10) had made their policing roles redundant.

HUNDRED BAILIFFS
Bailiffs were the Sheriff's officers, holding their bailiwicks from him at farm. They served his writs, executed his processes, arrested offenders and seized their goods, and took recognizances. They compiled jury lists, and summoned those required to appear at Quarter Sessions. Their work could be dangerous: the rolls of Durham Quarter Sessions record numerous instances of assault against them as they carried out their duties.[8]

Bailiffs were generally appointed for each Hundred; they were supposed to serve for one year only, although they could be re-appointed after three years. Sometimes, they were nominated, at the request of the Sheriff, by the freeholders of the Hundred.

INFORMERS
See Chapter 7

INSPECTORS OF WEIGHTS AND MEASURE
See Chapter 10.

JUSTICES' CLERKS
Many Justices had private clerks, who wrote their examinations, recognizances and other documents, and were paid by fees due to Justices. Justices' clerks attended Quarter Sessions even when their masters did not, in order to hand in the various documents produced by their principals between sessions.

As Petty Sessions developed in the eighteenth century, Justices appointed clerks jointly. They were frequently practising attorneys, and often also held other offices. Their fees were regulated in 1753. In 1851 Justices were given power to pay salaries; from 1877, fees were abolished and legal qualifications were required.

PARISH OFFICERS[9]

Churchwardens, overseers, constables and highway surveyors were, between them, responsible for many aspects of parish governance – relieving the poor, keeping the peace, maintaining the church and the highways and collecting taxes. They were expected to act as Justices directed. Constables and highway surveyors made presentments at Sessions; overseers were closely supervised by local Justices. Office holders were generally members of the parish elite immediately below the level of the gentry. They were frequently caught between the expectations of the Justices and the demands of good neighbourliness. But they were unpaid, non-professional, and frequently unwilling, holding office for one year only.

Poor Law overseers and highway surveyors were nominated by vestries, but appointed by Justices. Parish constables were manorial officers, but, after 1662, Justices of the Peace had the power of appointment where manorial courts had ceased to meet. The appointment of churchwardens was a matter for the church rather than for Justices.

PRISON GOVERNORS
See Chapter 10.

PROVOST MARSHALLS
The role of Provost Marshalls in the Militia, and in the apprehension of vagrants, was discussed in Chapter 1. In the 1630s, they were appointed under the Book of Orders as full-time paid officers, to administer the vagrancy laws. As such, they were much more effective than unpaid parish constables, although some commentators complained about their use of martial law.

REGISTRARS OF DEEDS
Deeds registries were established in Yorkshire and Middlesex in the early eighteenth century. Their registrars were elected, although generally the position was a sinecure; clerks were appointed to undertake the actual work. Elections were organised by Justices of the Peace; they are described in:
• Barber, Brian. 'A county election in miniature? Electing the Yorkshire registrars of deeds', *Yorkshire Archaeological Journal* 84, 2012, pp.160–87.

TREASURERS

Originally, Clerks of the Peace handled the finances of Quarter Sessions. However, as the task grew, separate treasurers began to be appointed in order to collect and disburse rates levied by parish constables. By the beginning of the eighteenth century, West Kent had treasurers for the bridge moneys, the gaol and vagrant monies, and the county stock. Treasurers were gentlemen, and sometimes Justices; they usually served for a year, and submitted accounts to Quarter Sessions. They were unpaid, but could invest moneys they held for their own advantage.

Business expanded inexorably in the late eighteenth century, and salaried treasurers began to be appointed. At first, their salaries were low: the treasurer of Lancashire, who had a balance of nearly £4,000 in his hands, was only paid £20 in 1798. By 1820, county treasurers were being paid perhaps £200 or £300 per annum.[10]

Chapter 7

TRADES AND OCCUPATIONS

Justices licenced and registered a variety of occupations, paid others, and recruited some (soldiers and seamen) themselves. Many registers, applications for licences, recognizances, and a variety of other records survive.

ALEHOUSE KEEPERS, INNKEEPERS, VICTUALLERS, ETC.

Sellers of intoxicating liquor have been licenced since 1552. All alehouse keepers (but not, initially, innkeepers – inns were substantial establishments catering for wealthy travellers) were supposed to be licenced. Generally, the task of licencing fell to the local Justices. The licensee entered into a recognizance promising not to permit 'unlawful games', not to harbour vagrants, and not to 'keep any disordered or evil rule in his house'.[1]

Restrictions on alehouse keepers were gradually extended; those who contravened them could lose their licences. No time period was specified in the 1552 Act, but the custom of annual licencing developed, reinforced by a Royal Proclamation in 1619. The two Justices granting a licence generally took into account two points: the conveniency of the house, and the character of the applicant. If he could find two sureties, the licence was likely to be granted.[2]

The 1552 Act was amended in 1729: licences were to be granted annually at special Petty or Brewster Sessions. Justices could only grant licences in their own divisions. The legislation was tidied up by a fresh Act in 1753, but not radically changed. The Alehouses Act of 1828 again tidied up the legislation, providing a new framework for licencing the sale of beer, wine, and spirits, and for regulating inns. After 1752, if premises were used for entertainment, that might require a separate licence (see below).

Licencing records consist primarily of recognizances and registers. Recognizances generally name the licensee, his parish and two sureties. The actual house or inn sign was unlikely to be mentioned until the late eighteenth century. Recognizances may be bound up separately in rolls or bundles, or included in the sessional rolls. They ceased to be required in 1828.

Records are sparse for the sixteenth century, although at least 297 recognizances were certified to the Somerset Quarter Sessions in 1630.[3] The proclamation of 1619 ordered Clerks of the Peace to keep annual registers of recognizances. Surviving registers mostly date from after 1753, when they were made statutory. The requirement did not last: the 1828 Act made no provision for registers of licencees. However, minutes, annual reports and correspondence of county licensing committees may be available for the succeeding period. The 1753 Act required prospective licensees to submit testimonials of good character, signed by their local minister and churchwardens. In Middlesex, constables made returns of victuallers and spirit retailers, giving names, whether licensed or unlicensed, the inn sign and sometimes the street. Similar returns are occasionally found elsewhere. Sessional rolls may include related documents, such as presentments, petitions and indictments relating to unlicensed or 'disorderly' houses, and lists of licenced premises. Order books may include similar documentation, as well as recording the grant of licences.

Constables were responsible for policing licensed premises. Their presentments sometimes dealt with matters such as unlicensed premises. Parish vestries also concerned themselves with their local alehouses.

Records of Brewster Sessions include similar documentation to that already discussed, although they are rare before the nineteenth century. The Licencing Act 1872 made it mandatory to keep registers of licences granted at Brewster Sessions. These are very detailed, including the name of the licensee, the inn sign and location, owner and leaseholder, the date the licence was first granted, the proximity of other licenced premises, and the type of customer, etc.

Licencing records for the final years of Quarter Sessions may sometimes be found amongst the archives of police forces. Licencing matters sometimes came before Assizes, so their records (see Chapter 12) may also contain relevant information.

Licencing was not just a local concern; it was also a matter for central government agencies. Late sixteenth-century wine licences, for example, were granted by letters patent, and subsequently by royal patentees. Between 1830 and 1869, beer house licences could be obtained from Excise offices. Full details of surviving records in The National Archives are given by Gibson's guide.

Further Reading
The history of alehouses is outlined in:
• Clark, Peter. *The English Ale House: Social History, 1200-1830.* (Longmans, 1983).

For an introduction to the records of licensees, see:
• Fowler, Simon. *Researching Brewery and Publican Ancestors.* (2nd ed. Family History Partnership, 2009).

For a detailed listing of the records, see:
• Gibson, Jeremy. *Victuallers' Licences: Records for Family and Local Historians.* (3rd ed. Family History Partnership, 2009).

See also:
• Tracing your ancestors who worked in pubs
www.pubhistorysociety.co.uk/PDF-Dowloads/ancestors.pdf

Dorset
• Dorset, England, Alehouse Licence, Records, 1754–1821
http://search.ancestry.co.uk/search/db.aspx?dbid=2216

ANNUITANTS
A 1762 Act required those claiming the right to vote by virtue of an annuity to take an oath, and certify the rent charge and the property from which it issued. Memorials submitted by annuitants to Clerks of the Peace may survive, as may the registers in which they were entered.

BADGERS, CHAPMEN, AND OTHER ITINERANTS
Badgers were itinerant sellers of corn, fish, butter and cheese. From 1563, they and other itinerant traders were licenced by Quarter Sessions. Recognizances and registers identify their homes and sureties.

Numbers licenced steadily declined in the eighteenth century, as both badgers and Justices increasingly ignored obsolescent legislation: badgers gradually became respectable businessmen. Licencing was abolished in 1772.

BARGE OWNERS
An Act of 1794 required vessels over 13 tons engaged in inland navigation to be registered by Clerks of the Peace. Certificates were issued to owners, and abstracts of registers sent to the Admiralty. Registers of barges record the kind of vessel, their burden, the names (and perhaps addresses) of owners and (usually) crewmen, the number of crew, the line of navigation, and the extent of the line of navigation. The requirement ceased in 1798, but sometimes registers were continued for a few years.

Registration was again imposed by the Canal Boat Acts of 1877 and 1884. Registers recorded names of owners and most masters, indicating the extent of accommodation for bargees' families on board. By 1883, 22,561 boats had been registered. Registration was conducted by Sanitary Authorities set up by the Local Government Board, and had nothing to do with Quarter Sessions.

Further Reading
Full details of both sets of registers are given in:
• Wilkes, Sue. *Tracing your Canal Ancestors: a Guide for Family Historians*. (Pen & Sword, 2011).

The evidence provided by the registers is used extensively in:
• Hanson, Harry. *The Canal Boat-men, 1760-1914*. (Manchester University Press, 1975).

BUTCHERS
During the sixteenth and seventeenth centuries, butchers were liable to fall foul of legislation prohibiting the eating of meat during Lent. They were sometimes required to enter into recognizances not to dress meat during this period. Such recognizances sometimes survive.

COMMON INFORMERS
Informations provided by common informers led to the prosecution of

many misdemeanours. Fines resulting from successful prosecution could be divided equally between the Crown and the informer. Informers could easily detect offences such as selling ale without a licence, trading without having served an apprenticeship, or building a cottage on less than four acres of land. In early seventeenth century Somerset individual informers presented up to forty informations at each sessions.[4]

By the end of the seventeenth century, some Justices had become suspicious of informers' activities. In the 1690s, several were presented for extortion at North Riding Quarter Sessions; its records cease to mention their activities after 1707.[5] By contrast, Essex informers were actually employed by Quarter Sessions; in 1719, they were formally instructed to investigate the whole range of offences triable by Quarter Sessions, and to make presentments.[6]

CORN DEALERS
Acts of 1791 and 1821 regulated corn imports and exports, requiring corn dealers, maltsters and millers buying corn for sale to make a declaration that they would make true returns of the price of corn. Declarations give names, abodes and occupations.

COWKEEPERS
An Order in Council made in 1879 required cowkeepers, dairymen and purveyors of milk to be registered. Registers record names, addresses, trades, and the conditions of their premises, especially their cleanliness. This order was related to action being taken to prevent the spread of contagious diseases amongst animals.[7]

ENTERTAINMENT
The Disorderly Houses Act of 1752 required houses used for dancing or other public entertainments in the London area to be licenced. Similar licences were required in the provinces from later in the century. Many papers from the Middlesex Sessions relating to these licences are held by London Metropolitan Archives. Licence applications, perhaps with petitions for or against the licence, were filed with Sessions papers until 1836; thereafter, there is a separate series, although only a few years survive. Some licences also survive. Documents name owners and addresses, and give the terms of licences. Printed lists of licences

A Cow Keeper in Golden Lane, London. (Courtesy of Wellcome Images.)

granted are held. Police reports from the 1860s and 1870s list applicants, addresses of premises and whether they were licensed to sell spirits. There are also police reports on the holders of music and dancing licences who sold spirits without a licence.

Under an Act of 1878, the Metropolitan Board of Works had to approve plans for alterations to places of entertainment; a few plans survive, together with letters certifying that work had been carried out according to approved plans.

FLAX AND HEMP GROWERS
Acts of 1763, 1781, and 1786 encouraged the growing of flax and hemp by granting bounties to growers. Claims noted the name of the

claimant, the land where the crop was grown and the amount claimed; they were counter-signed by a Justice and two parish officers. Receipts from dealers who had purchased the crop were sometimes attached. Claims were listed for presentation to Quarter Sessions, advertised, and then passed on to the Commissioners of Trades and Plantations. The Treasury remitted the cost to Quarter Sessions, who paid claimants. On receipt, claimants entered into bonds against false claims. Bonds give names, parishes, and occupations of growers and sureties, the quantity and location of flax grown, and the amount paid. Surviving records include original claims, lists of claimants, accounts and bonds.

GAMEKEEPERS AND THEIR EMPLOYERS

Many statutes restricted the killing of game to the elite. Possession of land worth over £100 per annum, or being the heirs of esquires and aristocrats, was required under an Act of 1670. This Act authorised the appointment of gamekeepers who could search the houses of suspected poachers, and seize nets, dogs, etc. From 1710, one gamekeeper from each manor had authority to kill game as the 'deputy' of his employer. Gamekeepers' deputations are recorded in registers. In some counties, these are found at the back of Quarter Sessions order books. Registers give the names of manors, their lords, and their gamekeepers, with dates. Gamekeepers were sometimes appointed for several manors; many were esquires, gentlemen, yeomen or even clergy. Registration continued into the twentieth century. These registers are useful sources for establishing the names of manorial lords, as well as enabling the careers of gamekeepers to be traced. Other records include original 'deputations', which may name witnesses, applications (or 'requisitions') for game certificates, and lists of those to whom certificates were issued.

William Parsons of Kirkby, gamekeeper drawn by Samuel Hieronymus Grimm, 1783.

Game duty, payable annually, was introduced in 1784; the Act required registers of persons qualified to kill game to be kept by the

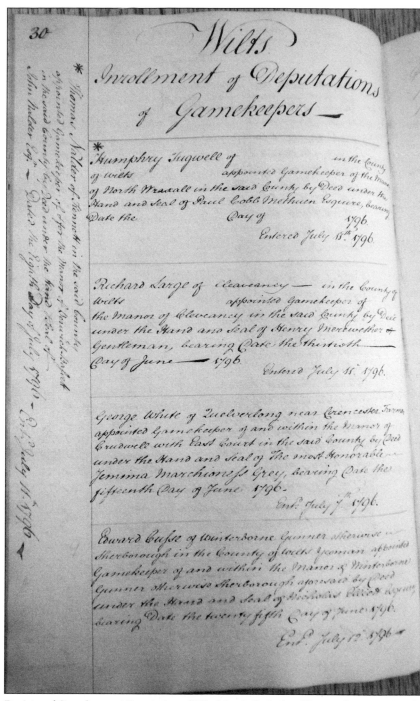

Wilts

Inrollment of Deputations of Gamekeepers —

* Humphry Tugwell of   in the County
of Wilts   appointed Gamekeeper of the Manor
of North Wraxall in the said County by Deed under the
Hand and Seal of Paul Cobb Methuen Esquire, bearing
Date the   Day of   1796.
Entered July 18th 1796.

Richard Large of Cleaveancy — in the County of
Wilts   appointed Gamekeeper of
the Manor of Cleaveancy in the said County by Deed
under the Hand and Seal of Henry Merewether &
Gentleman, bearing Date the thirtieth ——
Day of June —— 1796.
Entered July 18. 1796.

George White of Quelverlong near Cirencester Farmer
appointed Gamekeeper of and within the Manor of
Crudwell with East Court in the said County by Deed
under the Hand and Seal of The most Honorable
Jemima Marchioness Grey, bearing Date the
fifteenth Day of June 1796.
Entd July 7th 1796.

Edward Cusse of Winterborne Gunner otherwise
Sherborough in the County of Wilts Yeoman appointed
Gamekeeper of and within the Manor of Winterborne
Gunner otherwise Sherborough aforesaid by Deed
under the Hand and Seal of Nicholas Elliott Esquire
bearing Date the twenty fifth Day of June 1796.
Entd July 12th 1796 —

*Thomas Salter of Bennett in the said County
Appointed Gamekeeper if of for the Manor of Bennett Aforesaid
in the said County by Deed under the Hand & Seal of
John Barker Esqr. — Dated the Eighth Day of July 1796 — Entd July 18 1796

Register of Gamekeepers' Deputations. (Wiltshire & Swindon History Centre A1/307.)

Clerk of the Peace. They and their gamekeepers received game duty certificates. Sometimes separate registers for gentlemen and gamekeepers survive; these are quite distinct from the registers under the 1710 Act. Administration was transferred to the Collectors of Assessed Taxes in 1807.

MAIMED SOLDIERS

Soldiers injured during sixteenth-century and later wars were entitled to pensions. Applicants produced certificates testifying to their service and disability, and were examined by Justices of the Peace as to their impotency, loyalty, and indigence. Pensions were granted by Quarter Sessions, who raised a maimed soldiers' rate, and determined amounts. Officers received more. After the Restoration, Parliamentary soldiers were ineligible. The amount available was limited; applicants sometimes had to wait until a pension became available. In the meantime, they relied on the overseers. In Devon, Quarter Sessions refused to make grants unless the claimant received relief from his parish's overseers.[8] Many records survive, especially for Civil War casualties.

Order books record grants of pensions. Clerks of the Peace received petitions for relief, with supporting letters from commanders, and kept books listing maimed soldiers. Treasurers' accounts may also name them.

PRINTERS

The Unlawful Societies Act of 1799 required printers of 'irreligious, treasonable and seditious' papers to be suppressed. All printers needed a certificate from Clerks of the Peace, and submitted 'printers notices' giving their names, signatures, addresses and the number of presses. Witnesses and their addresses may also be named. The Clerk registered these notices, sending copies to the Secretary of State. Notification ceased to be required in 1869.

SEAMEN

Various Acts passed between 1794 and 1797 required Justices to recruit seamen, specifying numbers required from each county. A specially called General Sessions decided numbers required from each parish. The principal inhabitants selected recruits, and parish officers returned their names to Petty Sessions. Parishes levied rates to pay bounties;

advances could be paid to 'volunteers'. Records may list recruits, the parishes for which they served (not necessarily the same as parishes of settlement), their calling, age and the bounty paid to them. Treasurers' accounts may provide useful information.

SERVANTS

Justices of the Peace had jurisdiction over the relationship between master and servant from the fourteenth century. They fixed wages (see Chapter 10), punished those who broke covenants, and adjudicated when wages were not paid. In Somerset, early seventeenth-century complaints from masters and servants were regularly directed to Quarter Sessions, and as regularly referred back to two local Justices.[9]

The Statute of Artificers required servants in most trades to serve for at least a year, and to produce testimonials from their previous master when taking service with a new one. Masters who did not demand these testimonials could be prosecuted.[10] The penalty for departing from one's master without proper notice was imprisonment, frequently in Houses of Correction (see Chapter 10).

Between 1607 and 1611 a substantial number of offenders against these requirements, both masters and servants, were prosecuted in the North Riding. Three centuries later, Black Country industrialists were able to use the law against servants breaking their contracts when dealing with major strikes.[11]

The Statute of Artificers also made it an offence for those able to work to refuse to accept a master. Masterless men were regarded with suspicion, and frequently proceeded against. A statute of 1572 classified them as vagrants liable to punishment (see Chapter 8). Acceptance of casual work for a few days every month did not count; service had to be for at least a year. Quarter Sessions order books are full of orders requiring masterless men – especially teenagers – to find masters. Idle and potentially rowdy young people needed discipline to prevent them committing offences such as rioting.

Hundred Courts held annual hiring sessions, where wage rates were proclaimed, disputes between masters and servants arbitrated, returns listing servants and their wages from parish constables received, and agreements between masters and servants registered (the registers very occasionally survive). Masters were expected to attend these sessions; in 1676, no less than 120 masters were presented at Quarter Sessions for the Parts of Holland (Lincolnshire) for their failure to do so.[12] Hiring sessions mostly ceased during the eighteenth century.

SLAUGHTERHOUSE KEEPERS
Various Acts required slaughterhouses to be licenced. The earliest was an Act of 1786, aiming to reduce theft of cattle and horses. Subsequent Acts were concerned with hygiene and the prevention of diseases such as rinderpest. Registers were required under the Towns Improvement Clauses Act of 1847, the Public Health Act of 1848, and the Public Health Act of 1875. The slaughterhouse register of Chelmsford's Medical Officer of Health records dates of registration, addresses, names of owners and occupiers, descriptions of the animals killed, the numbers which may be slaughtered weekly and signatures of Clerks.

SOLDIERS (*see also* MAIMED SOLDIERS)
The Militia was the responsibility of the Lord Lieutenant (see Chapter 1). He sometimes obtained recruits amongst convicts at Quarter Sessions and Assizes. Justices of the Peace were given greater responsibility for recruitment by an Act of 1796. The same procedure was followed as is described above for the recruitment of seamen. London Metropolitan Archives holds relevant documents, including returns of 'volunteers' giving names, parishes, ages, occupations and the amount to be paid as bounty. It is noticeable that none of the men were settled in the parish for which they served; many were Irish.

SWEEPS
The Chimney Sweepers' Act of 1875 prevented young children from being employed as sweeps. It required sweeps to register their names with the police and to obtain licences. If they compelled children to climb chimneys, their licence would be revoked. Sweeps' registers record their names and addresses, with the names and ages of their employees, and may be found amongst police records in local record offices.

Chapter 8

PAUPERS, VAGRANTS AND LUNATICS

PAUPERS

As the population expanded during the sixteenth century, so did poverty. Increasing numbers of vagrants alarmed governments: poverty, vagrancy, masterlessness and landlessness all seemed to threaten the social order. And the abolition of monasteries and chantries, which had previously offered some relief to the poor, did not help.

I don't give to idlers.

The Poor Law Acts of 1597 and 1601 provided the official remedy for over two centuries. Under them, parish overseers provided work, relieved the impotent, bound pauper children as apprentices and levied parochial poor rates when necessary. Churchwardens were *ex officio* overseers. The records of overseers are parish records.[1]

Justices of the Peace appointed overseers on the nomination of parish vestries, examined their accounts and supervised their work. Between 1597 and 1834, this task occupied much of their time. They adjudicated disputes between paupers and overseers, between overseers and ratepayers, and between parishes. Justices had to be careful: paupers knew what their legal rights were, and did everything they could to exert them. The paupers of Potterne (Wiltshire), 'a very discontented and turbulent race', even clubbed together to purchase a copy of Burn's *Justice of the Peace and Parish Officer*, to inform themselves of their entitlements.[2]

Justices could grant habitation orders, requiring overseers to provide the poor with accommodation. They determined places of settlement, made removal orders, authorised the binding of pauper apprentices and conducted bastardy examinations to determine the parentage of bastards. Bastardy orders made by Justices required fathers to pay maintenance, either to the mother or to the overseers, until the child reached the age of seven, that is, until he could be apprenticed. Bastards' parents – especially their mothers – were frequently whipped.

The Elizabethan system, in its essentials, lasted for more than two centuries. When it was replaced in 1834, Justices continued to have some responsibilities. They served as guardians in the new Unions, continued to determine settlement, approved rates, adjudicated over emergency relief and settled disputes. Pauper lunatics (see below) continued to be admitted to asylums under Justices' control. Nevertheless, the 1834 Act contributed to the erosion of Justices' powers which we have already seen in the courts, and which also followed the introduction of professional policing.

The Elizabethan Acts provided that paupers were to receive relief from the parish in which they were 'settled'. Broadly, they could claim settlement by birth, by apprenticeship, by service for more than one year, by serving as a parish officer or by having paid rates on property valued at more than £10. The concept of 'settlement' received ever more precise definition after the 1662 Act of Settlement, and led to numerous disputes between parishes. The law of settlement has been described as 'that monstrous entanglement of statutes, amendments, and judgments . . . which . . . brought so much grist to the mill of the country attorney'.[3]

Justices' involvement in the process began when two of them examined paupers (or sometimes merely those thought likely to be paupers in future) to determine their settlement. Settlement examinations record the information given. They provide somewhat biased mini-biographies. Paupers' movements since they last gained settlements are recorded, but examinations ignore details irrelevant to their purpose. They may record names, ages, places of birth, details of parents, wives, children, and former masters, former places of residence and details of any apprenticeships served.

Once settlement had been determined, a removal order could be issued. These might be written on the backs of settlement examinations, although sometimes printed forms were used. They were usually acted upon immediately, and should have been signed by the constable of each parish through which the pauper passed. They give personal details of paupers, perhaps including names of wives and children. Examinees who were not actually claiming relief could obtain a settlement certificate from their home parish. These certificates acknowledged that parish's liability to pay relief if needed, and enabled its holder to avoid removal.

Settlement examinations, removal orders and settlement certificates, were generally kept in parish chests, either of the parish which secured removal, or of the parish of settlement. The latter, however, frequently appealed against removal orders which imposed a liability on them. Between 1700 and 1749, there were 581 appeals to the North Riding Quarter Sessions.[4] Quarter Sessions order books are full of decisions on such cases. Related settlement examinations and removal orders can frequently be found amongst Quarter Sessions records.

On arrival in his parish of settlement, the pauper was entitled to claim relief, including the provision of housing, food, fuel and/or clothing. Justices were expected to ensure relief was provided; paupers frequently appealed to Justices against overseers' decisions.

Justices also oversaw the apprenticing of pauper children. Apprenticeship was a respectable institution; it provided for the training of young men in a trade which would enable them to obtain a reasonable livelihood. Private apprentices normally spent seven years living in their masters' household whilst they learnt their trade; their parents sometimes paid substantial premiums to masters who could provide good training. Pauper apprenticeship was a perversion of this system; it provided a means by which overseers could exercise social control over the most volatile section of the community, and, at the same time, considerably reduce the impact of paupers on the poor rates. Overseers bound boys until they attained the age of 24 (reduced to 21 in 1778), without reference to their parents. Girls served until age 21 or marriage. Overseers could require masters in their own parish to accept parish apprentices, or could pay a small premium to masters outside of their parish. The cost of supporting pauper children was thus passed to their masters. The trades to which paupers were apprenticed were of low status – perhaps husbandry, or, for girls, housewifery – and frequently constituted mere drudgery. Sometimes, training was minimal. The terms of apprenticeship were recorded in pauper apprenticeship indentures, which overseers frequently retained in the parish chest.

Justices supervised apprenticeship. Apprenticeship disputes – both private and pauper – were amongst the commonest cases to come before individual justices. Edmund Tew's justicing book is full of references to them.[5] So are Quarter Sessions order books. Justices adjudicated complaints raised by both masters and apprentices, fined masters who refused to accept pauper apprentices, and punished apprentices who absconded. Masters needed Justices' approval to dismiss an apprentice, or to 'turn him over' to a new master. Justices re-assigned apprentices whose masters had died, been imprisoned for debt or gone out of business.

From 1802, Justices' assent to pauper bindings were recorded in registers of pauper apprentices kept by overseers. The Parish Apprentices Act of 1816 required Justices 'to enquire into the propriety of binding such child apprentices to the person or persons to whom it shall be proposed by . . . overseers to bind such child'; they had to sign a binding order, which was attached to the indenture.

The Elizabethan Poor Law was replaced by the New Poor Law Act in 1834. It merged many parishes into Poor Law Unions, governed by elected Boards of Guardians responsible to the central Poor Law Commissioners, not to Quarter Sessions. Unions were abolished in

1929. Their records are not county records, and are consequently outside of the scope of this book.

Further Reading
For good general introductions to the history of the Poor Law, see:
- Hindle, Steve. *On the Parish? The Micro-politics of Poor Relief in Rural England c1550-1750*. (Clarendon Press, 2004).
- Lees, Lynn Hollen. *The Solidarities of Strangers: The English Poor Laws and the People, 1700-1948*. (Cambridge University Press, 1998).

On the law of settlement, see:
- Taylor, J.S. *Poverty, Migration and Settlement in the Industrial Revolution: Sojourner's Narratives*. (Society for the Promotion of Science and Scholarship, 1989).

Basic introductions to Poor Law records are provided by:
- Fowler, Simon. *Poor Law Records for Family Historians*. (Family History Partnership, 2011).
- Cole, Anne. *Poor Law Documents before 1834*. (2nd ed. Federation of Family History Societies, 2000).

For a more detailed guide, see:
- Burlison, Robert. *Tracing Your Pauper Ancestors: A Guide for Family Historians*. (Pen & Sword, 2009).

Many facsimiles of Poor Law documents are printed in:
- Hawkings, David T. *Pauper Ancestors: A Guide to the Records Created by the Poor Laws in England and Wales*. (History Press, 2011).

Guides to settlement papers and overseers' accounts are included in:
- Thompson, K.M. *Short Guides to Records. Second Series Guides 25-48*. (Historical Association, 1997).

For a detailed guide to apprenticeship records (including pauper indentures), see:
- Raymond, Stuart A. *My Ancestor was an Apprentice: How Can I Find Out More about Him?* (Society of Genealogists, 2010).

For pauper letters, see:
- King, Steven. 'Pauper letters as a source', *Family & Community History* 10(2), 2007, pp.167–70.
- Levene, Alysa et al., eds. *Narratives of the Poor in Eighteenth-century Britain. Vol. 1: Voices of the Poor: Poor Law Depositions and Letters.* (Routledge, 2006).

The minutes of Poor Law Union guardians are described by:
- Coleman, Jane M. 'Guardians minute books', in Munby, Lionel M., ed. *Short Guides to Records.* (Historical Association, 1972, separately paginated).

An extensive listing of surviving union records is included in:
- Gibson, Jeremy, et al. *Poor Law Union Records.* (2nd/3rd eds. 4 vols. Federation of Family History Societies/Family History Partnership, 1997–2014).

A historical account of every workhouse, together with much other valuable information, is provided by:
- The Workhouse
  www.workhouses.org.uk/

See also:
- Reid, Andy. *The Union Workhouse: A Study Guide for Teachers and Local Historians.* (Phillimore, for the British Association for Local History, 1994).

Essex
- Sokoll, Thomas, ed. *Essex Pauper Letters, 1731-1837.* (Records of Social and Economic History, new series 30. Oxford University Press, 2001).

Gloucestershire
- Gray, Irvine, ed. *Cheltenham Settlement Examinations, 1815-1826.* (Bristol & Gloucestershire Archaeological Society Records Section 7, 1969).

Hampshire
• Willis, Arthur J., ed. *Winchester Settlement Papers 1667-1842, from Records of several Winchester Parishes*. (The author, 1967).

Lancashire
• Hindle, G. B. *Provision for the Relief of the Poor in Manchester 1754-1826*. (Chetham Society 3rd series 23, 1976). Useful bibliography.

Middlesex
• Hitchcock, Tim, & Black, John, eds. *Chelsea Settlement and Bastardy Examinations, 1733-1766*. (London Record Society 33, 1999).

Sussex
• Pilbeam, Norma, & Nelson, Ian, eds. *Poor Law Records of Mid-Sussex 1601-1835*. (Sussex Record Society 83, 1999).

Wiltshire
• Hembry, Phyllis, ed. *Calendar of Bradford on Avon Settlement Examinations and Removal Orders 1725-98*. (Wiltshire Record Society 46, 1990).

VAGRANTS

Vagrancy was another important issue for the Justices, especially in the sixteenth and seventeenth centuries. Vagrants were defined as poor, able-bodied men and women without employment or fixed abode. The law required them to find masters or face punishment. The government viewed the problem of vagrancy very seriously. In late sixteenth-century Warwick, the main judicial business was vagrancy. Between 1631 and 1639, there were almost 25,000 convictions for the crime of vagabondage.[6] The role of Provost Marshalls in dealing with vagrants was noted in Chapter 6.

The term 'vagrant' was very imprecise, and meant whatever an individual Justice wanted it to mean. Many were charged with deserting or failing to maintain their families. Prostitutes could be charged as vagrants, although prostitution itself was not illegal. Servants who absconded from their masters were regarded as vagrants. Other minor crimes frequently resulted in a charge of vagrancy, since prosecution was much easier: individual Justices had summary jurisdiction and no jury was required. Justices could order a whipping or incarceration in the House of Correction. A charge of vagrancy could also mitigate the sentence that a more serious charge might incur. Conversely, some suspects committed as vagrants were subsequently found guilty on different charges.

Legally, paupers and vagrants were distinct, although in practice they were frequently identical. They were dealt with by parish officers, and their treatment became increasingly similar. The Vagrant Removal Cost Act of 1700 removed the costs of vagrant administration from parishes to counties, and had the unintentional effect of encouraging parishes to treat paupers (for whom they were liable) as vagrants. Parishes were thus enabled to reduce their costs.

Prejudice against itinerants amongst the settled population was

Whipping at the cart's tail, from Mark Twain's The Prince and the Pauper.

"THE WERE WHIPPED AT THE CART'S TAIL."

Wilts to Wit

Vagrant

The Examination of John Brooks of [illegible] taken before

[illegible] the Eighth day of Aug.t 1740 in [illegible]

This Examin.t Saith That he was born at [illegible]

That he was afterwards bound an Apprentice to our John

Galloday of Tidlyth in the County of Cornwall for [illegible]

Terme of Seven Years That to Serve with the Whole Terme —

Of an Apprentice to the s.d John Galloday at Tidlyth

aforesd That being afterwards Impresd into the

Service of the late Queen Ann And Continued

in the Service for four Years or thereabout Was then Discharged?

[illegible] in the Year 1713. And that for 26 Years past

was cast part of his Revenue Was taken up King of [illegible]

Downe that part of Great Britain Called England e Work?

at his Trade or Craft or to Work Able to Work

John Brooks

Duly Sworn e Examine?
at [illegible] in the Parish
of Wilts aforesd On the Day
e Year about Afore sd

[signatures]
Geo. Willoughby.

This Examinat of John Brooks One of his
Mr. Buxton aboue named that Brooks has upon Oath
On the Day e Year about

This Examinat Saith That he was born at [illegible] Eight aboutsd?
And has Served? e bound to Work with his Father four Years Be
Was Able to do any Work belonging to the Trade of [illegible]

John Brooks

Duly Sworn e Examine?
at [illegible] about On the
Day e Year about afore sd

[signatures]
Geo. Willoughby.
Tho. Buxton.

The vagrant examination of John Brooks. (Wiltshire & Swindon History Centre A1/330.)

strong; they were feared. Justices could grant passes to itinerants such as soldiers returning from wars (for whom no other provision was made), shipwrecked mariners or poor students travelling to or from University. Effectively, these were licences to beg, and were frequently counterfeited. Not all vagrants had a pass, and punishment for vagrancy could be harsh. Conviction might mean a whipping, and mutilation of one's ear. A third conviction was a felony, subject to hanging. Incarceration in either a prison or a House of Correction was frequent, as was impressment into the army or Royal Navy.

Once punishment had been inflicted, vagrants were 'passed' to their parish of 'settlement', accompanied by constables. Between 1700 and 1739 separate rates were sometimes levied to pay for passing. Vagrants' passes were similar to pauper removal orders, but were directed to constables, rather than to overseers and churchwardens.

Documentation of vagrancy improved in the early eighteenth century, largely as a result of the Act of 1700 mentioned above, and of the Vagrant Act of 1714. The latter required Justices to record examinations of vagrants in duplicate, to lodge one copy with the Clerk of the Peace, and to either make a warrant for committal to the House of Correction, or issue a pass to convey the vagrant to his/her parish of settlement. Passes could only be issued after examination, and after a whipping (although many Justices ignored the latter). Parish constables received certificates specifying the mode of travel, and the route, and returned them with their claims for expenses to county Treasurers. Their claims listed vagrants conveyed, the routes used, and expenses such as subsistence costs for sick vagrants, burial and lying in costs, horse hire and charges for guards. Some counties appointed contractors to undertake the work; their expenses were similarly detailed.

Further Reading
For early modern vagrants, see:
• Beier, A.L. *Masterless Men: the Vagrancy Problem in England 1560-1642*. (Methuen, 1985).

Eighteenth-century vagrancy is considered in:
• Eccles, Audrey. *Vagrancy in Law and Practice under the Old Poor Law*. (Ashgate, 2012).

PAUPER AND OTHER LUNATICS

An Act of 1714 authorised Justices of the Peace to commit persons 'of little or no estates, who, by lunacy or otherwise are furiously mad, and dangerous to be permitted to go abroad'. This was re-enacted in 1744. These Acts probably codified existing practice. Pauper lunatics could be confined in workhouses, or in Houses of Correction. An 1807 enquiry counted 2,398 pauper lunatics; 1,765 were in workhouses, 113 in Houses of Correction. Presumably the rest stayed with their families.[7]

Better provision was authorised by the County Asylums Act of 1808. The first asylum under this Act was opened in Nottinghamshire in 1812. Provision was not, however, compulsory, and Kent's first asylum was not opened until 1833. It was not until 1845 that Justices were required to build asylums, which were to be subjected to regular Home Office inspection. Essex opened its first asylum in 1853.

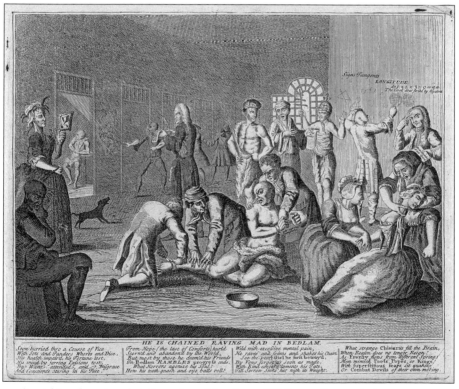

An eighteenth-century lunatic asylum. (Courtesy of Wellcome Images.)

Admittance to county asylums was authorised by a Justice on application by a parish overseer, or, after 1834, a Union relieving officer. Magisterial control over admittances continued until as late as 1959, subject to various checks from professionals. From 1845, when a medical officer or a constable became aware of a pauper lunatic, he had to notify the relieving officer within three days. He, in turn, brought the lunatic before a Justice of the Peace within three days. Union medical officers signed applications for admission after 1853. Justices had discretion over admittances, and could admit lunatics who had come to their notice in other ways – as when David Perkins heaved a brick through a Leicestershire Justice's window in 1851![8] After 1853, if a patient had certificates from both the medical officer and an independent doctor, he or she had to be admitted.

County asylums were almost completely ignored by the 1834 Poor Law Act, remaining under the control of Quarter Sessions. Provision was insufficient to keep up with demand; asylums rapidly became overcrowded. Some pauper lunatics stayed in workhouses; others were returned there from overcrowded asylums. Union medical officers, under an 1862 Act, could determine whether a lunatic was 'a proper person to be kept in a workhouse'.

By Acts of 1815 and 1828, parish overseers were required to make returns of pauper lunatics to Clerks of the Peace. These state patients' names, ages, how long they had been ill, and the cost of their maintenance. After 1842, similar returns were made by the clerks of Poor Law Unions to the Poor Law Commissioners; these are now in The National Archives, series MH 12, and selected records can be downloaded.

County asylum records include papers relating to their establishment and maintenance. Quarter Sessions appointed Visitors, whose minutes and reports may be available. So may admission registers, case books, reports from medical officers, personnel records, registers of deaths and burials, title deeds, and a variety of other documents. The records of Lancaster Asylum include committal warrants, 1816–63, and a diet book for 1883–9. Asylums had to make returns of patients under the 1815 Act. After 1845, copies of admission registers of both public and private asylums had to be sent to the Lunacy Commission; they are now in The National Archives, series MH 94, and are digitised at http://search. ancestry.co.uk/search/db.aspx?dbid=9051; The Commissioners also received information on asylum building plans, now in series MH 83. The *Report of the Metropolitan Commissioners in Lunacy to the Lord Chancellor* (1844) is a detailed account of the condition of every asylum in England and Wales.[9]

Admission documents may prove particularly useful to researchers for biographical purposes. Their content was prescribed under Acts of 1845 and 1853. Justices had to certify that the patient was a proper candidate for admission to the Asylum. They did, however, have to be convinced by both relieving officers and medical officers, who both provided much useful information.

Asylum case books were not prescribed by legislation until 1845, but were frequently kept. The printed case books for Leicestershire provided space for entering basic personal information, plus various medical questions with spaces for answers.[10]

Justices also had responsibilities towards lunatics who were not paupers. The Madhouses' Act of 1774 (and a subsequent Act of 1832) required Quarter Sessions to licence private asylums; Justices were to be appointed as visitors, except in London, where this role was performed by the College of Physicians. Admittance required certification by a physician, surgeon, or apothecary. Names of inmates were certified to the College of Physicians until 1828, and to the Home Secretary until 1845 (although records cannot now be traced). Prior to the Asylum Act of 1845, there were generally more pauper inmates than private patients. Paupers were not, however, admitted if there was room for them in a county asylum. An 1815 Act permitted private patients to be admitted to county asylums if there was space. Further regulations were introduced by Acts of 1828 and 1845.

Applications for madhouse licences, plans of buildings, registers of admissions, visitors' report books and other records may survive amongst Quarter Sessions archives. Annual reports and minutes of visitors may also be found. A register of private asylums for 1798–1812, with the names of patients admitted, is in The National Archives, MH 51/735. Records from various private asylums are currently being digitised by the Wellcome Library (http://wellcomelibrary.org/collections/digital-collections/mental-healthcare). The records of many asylums, both public and private, are listed in the Hospital Records Database (www.nationalarchives.gov.uk/hospitalrecords).

Further Reading

The best introduction to the history of madness is:

• Scull, Andrew. *The Most Solitary of Afflictions: Madness and Society in Britain, 1700-1900*. (Yale University Press, 1993).

See also:

• Bartlett, Peter. *The Poor Law of Lunacy: the Administration of Pauper Lunatics in mid-nineteenth-century England*. (Leicester University Press, 1999).
• Smith, Leonard D. *Cure, Comfort and Safe Custody: Public Lunatic Asylums in early nineteenth-century England*. (Leicester University Press, 1999).

A detailed guide to lunatic records is provided by:

• Chater, Kathy. *My Ancestor was a Lunatic*. (Society of Genealogists Enterprises, 2015).

Chapter 9

RELIGION

Religion was a matter for the ecclesiastical courts, which exercised a wide jurisdiction in matters of 'sin, sex, and probate', as one author has put it. Nevertheless, some ecclesiastical matters came before Quarter Sessions and individual Justices. The earliest relevant legislation was passed in 1414, when Justices were asked to help eradicate the Lollard 'heresy'. In the sixteenth and seventeenth centuries, Lord Lieutenants were active in rooting out Roman Catholicism. Division in the church meant division in the state: consequently, the Crown demanded uniformity in religion, especially during the Reformation. Before 1688, the great bulk of the evidence for both Roman Catholics and Nonconformists derives from the efforts of church and state to compel them to conform to the established religion.

RECUSANCY
Attendance at church was the litmus test of theological correctness during and after the Reformation. Those refusing to attend were termed recusants. The word is derived from the Latin *recusare*, to reject. Recusants rejected the established church, and refused to attend it. Their refusal was seen as a rejection of royal authority.

Most recusants, at least before 1660, were Papists. Roman Catholicism was considered seditious after the Reformation, and therefore concerned Justices. The severity of the law, however, was rarely matched by severity in its execution, except during emergencies such as the Spanish Armada, the Gunpowder Plot and the Jacobite rebellions.

Protestant Nonconformity was almost as much of a problem. In the 1630s, the clash of Puritanism with Laudianism helped to pave the way for civil war. After the Restoration, over 2,000 non-conforming clergy were ejected from their livings. Their loyalty to the Crown was considered to be very questionable, and the Recusancy Acts were used against them. They were also subjected to the Conventicle Acts of 1664 and 1670, which prohibited non-Anglican religious gatherings, and imposed heavy fines on attenders. The 1664 Act required Justices to compile certificates of convictions for conventicle attenders; surviving certificates may record the names of entire congregations. John Bunyan fell foul of these Acts; his dialogues with Justices, with the Bedfordshire Clerk of the Peace, and with the Assize judges demonstrate their varying attitudes towards dissent.[1]

The Act of Uniformity of 1559 imposed a fine of 12d for refusal to attend Church of England services, leviable by churchwardens; the money was intended for poor relief. Initially, there were few prosecutions. However, the Northern Rising of 1569 and the Papal excommunication of Queen Elizabeth the following year led to an increasing volume of retaliatory legislation. An Act of 1581 (tightened up in 1586–7) made absence from church an indictable offence presentable at Quarter Sessions, raising the fine to a ruinous £20 per month.[2] Penalties could, however, be mitigated in the same way as other serious charges at Quarter Sessions: it was easy to alter indictments to change the stated period of recusancy from a month or more to a mere three weeks, thus lowering the potential fine to a mere three shillings.

Various other offences could bring Roman Catholics and dissenters before the courts, for example celebration or attendance at mass, reconciling Protestants, attendance at conventicles, educating children abroad at colleges such as Douai and Rheims, priest-harbouring, possession of Papist books, refusal of oaths, and objectionable outbursts. Such offences are documented by presentments and indictments (see Chapter 5). These become more numerous towards the end of Elizabeth's reign. In the seventeenth century, presentments became much commoner than indictments. Order books record actions taken against Catholic and dissenting communities as a whole, for example, searches for weapons, and orders to constables to be more rigorous in making presentments against them. In 1593, Lieutenants were instructed to certify the names of those attending overseas colleges, and to take bonds from parents for their appearance.[3]

It was the luck of the draw whether absence from church was presented to the Archdeaconry court by the churchwarden, or to Quarter Sessions by the constable. Sometimes, presentments were made to both: Richard Gaye of Keynsham (Somerset) was accused of

112

saying 'that the Queen's laws are not agreeable to God's laws', and presented for not coming to church at Bishop Still's visitation in 1594. In the same year, a presentment at Quarter Sessions reported that Gaye 'did not repaire' to the parish church.[4] Informers could also prosecute recusants in the Westminster courts.

The absence of presentments or indictments does not mean the absence of either Roman Catholics or dissenters in a particular parish. Many churchwardens and constables were themselves one or the other, or sympathetic to them. Justices themselves were frequently reluctant to enforce the penal statutes. In 1605, no less than 5,000 persons were prosecuted for recusancy, but only 112 paid the full legal penalty, i.e. two-thirds of the value of their estates.[5] During the Interregnum, there were no presentments for recusancy at any of the Yorkshire Quarter Sessions.[6] Conservative justices stymied efforts to move against them. In Lancashire, it took determined planning on the part of Puritan justices to obtain some action in a county dominated by the conservative Lord Derby. Lancashire's sessions were customarily adjourned from one place to another, and Justices normally attended only their local sessions. Puritan justices were concentrated in Salford Hundred. In 1579, they began attending sessions in other places, in a determined effort to pursue recusants. The result was the presentation of 600 recusants.[7] Presentments could also be made to Assize judges; the few made at Lancashire Quarter Sessions under the 1581 Act were counterbalanced by the large number made to the Assize judges at Lancaster.[8]

A variety of documents record recusancy, in addition to those already mentioned. Fines imposed by Quarter Sessions on recusants were recorded in the estreats sent to the Exchequer[9] by the Clerk of the Peace, and in the pipe rolls (National Archives, E 372/426-436). The relevant entries are abstracted in:

- McCann, T.J., ed. *Recusants in the Exchequer Pipe Rolls, 1581-1592* (Catholic Record Society 71, 1986).

In 1592, a new series of recusant rolls were commenced, continuing until 1691 (E 376-7; see also E 351 and E 370). They record fines levied and property confiscated for recusancy.[10] Most of those fined were Roman Catholics; however, many Nonconformists also suffered, especially after the Restoration. A number of rolls have been published by the Catholic Record Society http://catholicrecordsociety.co.uk. A useful introduction is included in:

- Bowler, Hugh, ed. *Recusant Roll No.2 (1593-1594)*. (Catholic Record Society 57, 1965).

Failure to pay the fines legislated for in 1581 could lead to imprisonment, details of which can be found in the records of Quarter Sessions and Assizes (see Chapters 5 and 12). After 1586, two-thirds of a recusant's land, and all his goods and chattels, could be confiscated. Accounts of shrieval seizures of recusant property are in The National Archives, E 379, as well as on the recusant rolls.

Although recusant rolls ended in 1691, Roman Catholicism continued to be seen as a serious threat, especially during the Jacobite rebellions. There is a draft 1745 warrant amongst the Cumberland Lieutenancy papers directing constables to 'seize the persons and arms of all papists', although whether it was executed is not clear.[11] Certainly, less drastic action was taken. Following the 1715 rebellion, Catholics were required to register their estates with the Clerk of the Peace, who made returns to the Exchequer (E 174). Other records of the rebellions can be found amongst the Forfeited Estates Commission archives (FEC 1-2).

A useful introduction to Catholic records is available on The National Archives' website:

- Catholic Recusants
  www.nationalarchives.gov.uk/help-with-your-research/research-guides/catholics

For recusant rolls, see:
- Williams, J. Anthony. 'Recusant rolls', in Munby, Lionel M. *Short Guides to Records*. (Historical Association, 1971) (separately paginated).

Abstracts of the 1715 returns are printed in:
- Estcourt, Edgar E. and Payne, John Orlebar, eds. *The English Catholic Non-Jurors of 1715*. (Burns & Oates, [1885]).

For forfeited Jacobite estates, see:
- *The Records of the Forfeited Estates Commission*. (HMSO, 1968).

OATHS OF ALLEGIANCE

The threat of Roman Catholicism and Nonconformity led the government to demand oaths of allegiance from all who held public office. Some were administered by the church, and recorded in diocesan records. Other oath records are amongst the archives of both Quarter Sessions and central government.

The Test Act of 1672[12] required civil and military office-holders to obtain sacrament certificates, confirming they had taken Holy Communion according to Anglican rites. These are amongst Quarter Sessions records, and in The National Archives, series C 224, KB 22, E 196, and CHES 4. Most of The National Archives' certificates (except those in CHES 4 for Cheshire) relate to the London region. Certificates give names of communicants, places, and signatures of ministers, churchwardens, and witnesses.

The Test Act also required office-holders to take the oaths of allegiance, supremacy and against the doctrine of transubstantiation. These oaths could be taken in the courts of King's Bench and Chancery, or at Quarter Sessions. Between 1689 and 1702, beneficed clergy, members of the universities, lawyers, schoolteachers and preachers also had to take these oaths. The Privy Council in the late seventeenth century regarded them as 'one of the most useful weapons in the arsenal of local government'.[13] After 1828, both sacrament certificates and oaths were abolished. Office holders merely had to declare that they would do nothing to damage the Church of England.

A variety of other oaths also had to be taken, and numerous rolls can be found amongst both Quarter Sessions records and in The National Archives. After the Restoration, the oath of allegiance was required of office holders and others; in some cases, whole parishes took it, as at Babington and Radstock (Somerset).[14] The oath of abjuration, under the Security of Succession Act of 1702, was a declaration of allegiance to Queen Anne, and of support for the Protestant succession. It was superseded by the Security of the Sovereign Act of 1714. Under the 1689 Toleration Act, dissenters had to take separate oaths of allegiance and supremacy, and make a declaration against transubstantiation. Dissenting clergy had to declare their acceptance of most of the articles of religion.

Following an attempt to assassinate William III, the Act of Association of 1695/6 required all office holders to swear an oath to defend the king. In practice, this oath was signed by most men of any social standing. Almost 500 rolls are now in The National Archives, series C 213, with a few in C 214 & KB 24/1-2. Some can also be found amongst Quarter Sessions records. The Lancashire rolls were edited by Wallace Gandy in *The Lancashire Association Oath Rolls, A.D. 1696* (Society of Genealogists, 1921).

In the aftermath of the Atterbury plot, a 1722 Act required men over the age of 18 years to take the oaths of allegiance by 25 December 1723 (subsequently extended until 28 November 1728) or to register their names and estates as papists. This was the last exercise in mass public oath-taking. In contrast to earlier oath rolls, many women signed. Also in contrast to earlier rolls, oaths were not necessarily tendered in the subscriber's parish or Hundred of residence. Rolls may, however, give places of residence and occupations. They are Quarter Sessions records. The Devon rolls for 1723 have been transcribed by the Friends of Devon Archives www.foda. org.uk/oaths/intro/introduction1.htm. A full listing of surviving English returns is available online.[15]

A Nonconformist minister. A print from the series of Cryes of the City of London Drawne after the Life, *published in 1687.*

After the Catholic Relief Act of 1778, Roman Catholics could free themselves from the penal laws by taking an oath of loyalty. Registers and returns are found amongst Quarter Sessions records, and in The National Archives, series PC 1. They may give domiciles and occupations as well as names. An Act of 1829 required members of Roman Catholic religious orders to be registered with the Clerk of the Peace. Applications for registration, and registers, may survive amongst Quarter Sessions records.

This discussion has not mentioned the Protestation and other Civil War oaths. These had nothing to do with Quarter Sessions.[16]

QUAKERS

Quakers refused to take oaths, and were punished for their refusal.

Records can be found in Quarter Sessions and Assize records, and compared with Quaker records. 'Sufferings' were recorded in the minutes of their Monthly Meetings (mostly now deposited in local record offices). Details were also sent to London, and recorded in the 'Great books of sufferings', and other records. These are now held at Friends House Library www.quaker.org.uk/library. Abstracts have been published in:

• Besse, Joseph. *Sufferings of Early Quakers*, ed. Michael Gandy. 10 vols. (Sessions Books, 1998–2008). Facsimile of 1753 edition.

After 1723, Quakers could affirm their loyalty, rather than taking an oath. Affirmation rolls can be found amongst Quarter Sessions records.

MEETING HOUSE LICENCES

The Declaration of Indulgence of 1672 authorised the granting of licences to dissenters. Although it was quickly abandoned, licencing was revived by the 1689 Toleration Act. Individuals could be licenced to preach. Meeting houses could also be licenced. Licences were issued by bishops, archdeacons and Quarter Sessions. Initially, most applications were made to Quarter Sessions, but they could only grant licences during their sessions. Consequently, the majority of licences were granted by ecclesiastical authorities. Petitions for licences, and registers of them, are described in:

• Welch, Edwin. 'The registration of meeting houses', *Journal of the Society of Archivists* 3, 1966, pp.116–20.

Licences issued under the 1672 Declaration of Indulgence can be found in The National Archives, series SP29/320-1, SP44/27, and SP44/33A-B. They are printed in:

• Turner, G.L., ed. *Original Records of Early Nonconformity under Persecution and Indulgence*. 3 vols (1911). Turner's work is supplemented by Nuttall, Geoffrey F., ed. 'Lyon Turner's *Original Records*: notes and identifications', *Transactions of the Congregational Historical Society* 14, 1940–4, pp.14–24, 112–20 & 181–7; 15, 1945–8, pp.41–7; 19, 1960–4, pp.160–4.

The Quaker Meeting House at Spiceland, Devon.

Nonconformist meeting house licences identify prominent dissenters, and the houses in which they met. They do not necessarily indicate denominational allegiances. Methodists in particular were prone to describe themselves as 'Protestant' or 'Independent'. Denominations may frequently be deduced from the names of petitioners, and/or from the survival of buildings.

Roman Catholic churches also had to be registered, initially under the Roman Catholic Chapels Act of 1791. Applications for registration are amongst Quarter Sessions archives, and may name priests. An Act of 1832 made Roman Catholics' places of worship subject to the same registration provisions as dissenters.

The Civil Registration Act of 1837 permitted Nonconformists to register chapels for the conduct of marriages.[17] The register was to be maintained by the Registrar General. This duplicated the registers which have already been described, so the two systems were united in 1852 by the Registrar-General's 'Worship register'. At the same time, all former licencing authorities made returns of meeting houses licenced since

118

1689, and also of Roman Catholic registrations since 1791. These are now in The National Archives, series RG31. They duplicate the registers already mentioned, but may be useful if the latter have been lost.

The Worship Register is ongoing. It is described in:

• Rose, R.B. 'Some national sources for Protestant Nonconformist and Roman Catholic history', *Bulletin of the Institute of Historical Research* 31, 1958, pp.79–83.

Abstracts of licences for a number of counties have been published. They do not necessarily abstract licences from all licencing authorities. Useful introductions can be found in:

Bedfordshire
• Welch, Edwin, ed. *Bedfordshire Chapels and Meeting Houses: Official Registration, 1672-1901.* (Publications of the Bedfordshire Historical Record Society 75, 1996).

Berkshire
• Spurrier, Lisa, ed. *Berkshire Nonconformist Meeting House Registrations, 1689-1852.* 2 vols. (Berkshire Record Society 9–10, 2005).

Staffordshire
• Donaldson, Barbara, ed. *The Registrations of dissenting chapels and meeting houses in Staffordshire 1689-1852: extracted from the return in the General Register Office made under the Protestant Dissenters Act of 1852 (15 and 16 Vic. c.36).* (Collections for a History of Staffordshire 4th series 3. Staffordshire Record Society, 1960).

Wiltshire
• Chandler, J.H., ed. *Wiltshire Dissenter's Meeting House Certificates and Registrations 1689-1852.* (Wiltshire Record Society 40, 1985).

RETURNS OF NON-ANGLICAN PLACES OF WORSHIP, 1829
Another official record of Nonconformist places of worship is provided by the returns which Clerks of the Peace made in response to a resolution of the House of Commons in 1829. Unfortunately, these were

destroyed by fire in 1834, but the return for Lancashire had been published,[18] and copies of returns for at least fifteen other counties were retained amongst Quarter Sessions records. Returns list places of worship and their denominations, and may include numbers and comments from incumbents. A detailed discussion is provided in:

- Ambler, R.W. 'A lost source? The 1829 returns of non-Anglican places of worship', *Local Historian* 17(8), 1987, pp.483–9.

See also:
- Tranter, Margery. 'Many and diverse dissenters: the 1829 returns for Derbyshire', *Local Historian* 18(4), 1988, pp.162–7.

FURTHER READING
- Shorney, David. *Protestant Nonconformity and Roman Catholicism: a guide to sources in the Public Record Office.* (PRO Publications, 1996).
- Williams, J. Anthony. *Sources for recusant history (1559-1791) in English official archives.* (*Recusant History* 16(4), 1983).

Chapter 10

THE COURT AS ADMINISTRATOR AND SUPERVISOR

ANIMAL DISEASES

Animal diseases have been subjected to regulation at least since the Act of 1745/6 'for preventing the spread of distemper among the horned cattle'. Under this Act, Justices appointed inspectors, reimbursed farmers who lost cattle, obtained reports from constables and undertook much other work. Inspectors' and constables' reports, accounts, orders and other documentation may survive.

The Cattle Diseases Prevention Act of 1866 followed a serious outbreak of rinderpest, and was followed by Acts of 1869 and 1878, dealing with swine fever and other animal diseases. Quarter Sessions were empowered to appoint inspectors, close markets, slaughter diseased animals, pay compensation and grant licences to transport cattle. Records include committee minutes, accounts, the reports of inspectors, lists of cattle slaughtered, forms for claiming compensation, vouchers for compensation paid, diseases of animals rate lists and miscellaneous correspondence. Orders may be recorded in Quarter Sessions order books. Reports of the Cattle Plague Commissioners can be found in the *Parliamentary Papers*.

BRIDGES

Bridge maintenance became the responsibility of Quarter Sessions under the Statute of Bridges of 1530/1, although they could determine that others bore that responsibility. Supervision of bridge repairs was generally assigned to local Justices. Costs were met by county-wide or local bridge rates, by tolls, or sometimes by charity. In the late eighteenth century, professional bridge surveyors began to be appointed.[1] In some counties, they conducted surveys of all county bridges, which provide useful information to local historians.

The packhorse bridge at Whaddon, Wiltshire, repaired by the county in 1856.

Bridges are frequently mentioned in Quarter Sessions order books and presentments. Bridge Committee minutes, surveyors' reports, surveys, plans, contracts, and other papers can also frequently be found.

Further Reading
• Harrison, David. *The Bridges of Medieval England: Transport and Society, 400-1800.* (Clarendon Press, 2004).

See also Chapter 6 of:
• Webb, Sidney, & Webb, Beatrice. *The Story of the King's Highway.* (Frank Cass & Co., 1963. Originally published 1913).

CARRIAGE RATES
In 1691, Parliament required Quarter Sessions to set the rates of land carriage which carriers could charge. In 1748, another Act required them to send copies of their annual assessments to the Clerks of the Peace of Westminster, Middlesex and Surrey. These copies are held in London

Metropolitan Archives and Surrey History Centre, duplicating the assessments in the relevant county record offices. These assessments have been used to trace the effect turnpike trusts had on the cost of carriage during the Industrial Revolution.[2]

CHARITY

Charitable collections prior to the nineteenth century were authorised in two ways: briefs, and protections. Briefs authorised by the Court of Chancery were distributed to the clergy throughout the country.[3] In order to obtain a brief, Quarter Sessions had to be petitioned to certify the cause. Quarter Sessions could alternatively issue 'protections', or 'letters of request', for collections to be made locally.

Briefs and protections may be recorded in order books. Their uses were identical: they authorised collections to support victims of fire and flood, to raise ransoms for men enslaved by Barbary pirates, to pay for churches needing rebuilding and for similar purposes.

It should also be noted that many individual Justices served as Commissioners for Charitable Uses (see Chapter 13).

COTTAGES

In Tudor and Stuart England, the cottages of the poor were frequently little more than wooden frames occupying minimal space, erected at minimal cost. In 1588/9, their erection was banned, subject to certain exemptions, unless they stood in four acres of land – the minimum thought necessary to support a family. Otherwise, it was thought that they would attract undesirables, who 'worked when they felt in the mood . . . poached and pilfered as opportunities arose', and would be likely to claim poor relief.[4]

Many cottagers found four acres unaffordable. Quarter Sessions, however, could override the legislation and licence building. Many licences are recorded in order books. Petitions for licences may also be found, perhaps accompanied by consents from manorial lords. Conditions were sometimes imposed; Justices could, for example, require cottages to be removed after the petitioner's death, or specify the dimensions of the building. Dorset Justices frequently licenced cottages on condition that they became parish poor houses after their builders' deaths.[5]

Enforcement was sporadic. Many of the poor erected cottages without licences, hoping that Justices would allow buildings to remain. Sometimes they did, but they were just as likely to order immediate demolition. The Act was repealed in 1775.

COUNTY PROPERTY

Quarter Sessions owned various properties, which had to be maintained. Until c.1760, construction expenditure was fairly low, and mostly on bridges. Thereafter, expenditure soared. New buildings were necessitated by the increasing use of custodial sentences for crime, the prison reform movement, the need for lunatic asylums, Parliamentary directives and Assize orders. Houses of Correction, prisons, lunatic asylums and bridges are considered separately in this chapter and in Chapter 8. Shire halls, court buildings, judges' lodgings and police stations were also needed.

Quarter Sessions archives contain many relevant documents. Order books frequently refer to the building and maintenance of county property. Title deeds record the purchase of property, and may outline their previous history. Contracts identify contractors, and perhaps workmen. Accounts record how money was raised and spent.

Finance was frequently raised by imposing a special rate. Loans might also be raised, especially after 1784, when an Act relating to gaols and Houses of Correction gave Justices permission to borrow. Loans could be obtained from the Public Works Loan Commissioners, whose loan application registers from 1811 are in The National Archives (PWLB 6). Mortgage deeds may also record loans. Property could be leased, rather than purchased. Essex leased a room at Colchester Castle which served as a depot for the arms of the Eastern Essex Battalion of the Militia; there are leases dated 1837 and 1850.[6]

Controversial new buildings were sometimes the subject of litigation. A case concerning the provision of sick quarters in the new Essex county gaol between 1789 and 1792 produced eighteen bundles of documents, including opinions of counsel, briefs, reports, and other papers.[7]

Further Reading
- Chalklin, C. *English Counties and Public Building, 1650-1830.* (Hambledon Press, 1998).

DEEDS

The Statute of Enrolment of 1536 modified the feoffment, the ancient method of conveying land. The archaic ceremony of livery of seizin (in which a clod of earth was given by the vendor to the purchaser) was replaced by the enrolment of deeds of bargain and sale. Deeds had to be enrolled within six months of signing. Enrolment offered greater security of title.

Deeds were enrolled either in one of the Westminster courts (especially on Chancery's Close rolls, National Archives series C 54), or by Clerks of the Peace. Original deeds may be annotated with the date of enrolment. Enrolment was, however, patchy; in Devon, 1,300 deeds were enrolled in the late sixteenth century. By contrast, Essex only had 100 enrolments between 1536 and 1624. Lawyers disliked the publicity involved in enrolment, and devised means of evading the requirement.[8] There were few enrolments in the eighteenth century, although enclosure deeds continued to be enrolled with Clerks of the Peace until the General Enclosure Act of 1845. In a few counties, responsibility for enrolment was transferred to Deeds Registries in the eighteenth century.

Enrolled deeds provide valuable evidence on changes in landownership, including the disposal of former monastic and chantry land following their dissolution. They may also provide us with detailed descriptions of property in towns, and record field names not recorded elsewhere.

Further Reading

- Bates Harbin, Sophia W., ed. *Somerset Enrolled Deeds*. (Somerset Record Society 51, 1936).
- Sheppard, F., & Belcher, V. 'The deeds registries of Yorkshire and Middlesex', *Journal of the Society of Archivists* 6(5), 1980, pp.274–86.

ENCLOSURE

Enclosure of the open fields transformed eighteenth-century English landscapes. It also transformed the relative statuses of landowners, labourers and clergy. Common rights and communal farming ceased; farming became an individualistic enterprise; labourers were pauperised; clergy were gentified by being given land in exchange for tithes.

A typical enclosure landscape near Yeovil (Somerset), showing regularly-shaped fields.

Most enclosure was by Parliamentary Act. Between 1604 and 1914, over 5,000 enclosure Bills were enacted. They required the deposit of awards and maps with both the Clerk of the Peace, and in the parish chest. These documents list landowners, and detail the allocation of land for both private and public use. They record the shapes and sizes of the fields, and show how new roads were to be laid out.

Enclosure documents can now be found in county record offices. After 1845, they can also be found in The National Archives, series MAF 1. Sometimes they are accompanied by the relevant Act, which can also be found in the Parliamentary Archives at www.parliament.uk/business/publications/parliamentary-archives.

Further Reading
For a detailed guide to enclosure records, see:
• Hollowell, S. *Enclosure Records for Historians.* (Phillimore, 2000).

Acts and awards are listed in:
• Tate, W.E. *Domesday of English Enclosure Acts and Awards,* ed. M.E. Turner. (University of Reading Library, 1978).

Enclosure maps are catalogued in:
• Kain, Roger J.P., Chapman, John, & Oliver, Richard. *The Enclosure Maps of England and Wales, 1595-1918.* (Cambridge University Press, 2004). This includes an online database at http://hds.essex.ac.uk/em/

For enclosure records at The National Archives, see:
• Enclosure Awards
www.nationalarchives.gov.uk/help-with-your-research/research-guides/enclosure-awards

For Wales, see:
• Chapman, John. *Guide to Parliamentary Enclosures in Wales.* (University of Wales Press, 1992).

FREEMASONS
The Unlawful Societies Act of 1799, which suppressed certain 'dangerous' societies, exempted Freemasons' lodges on condition that they annually certified members' names, with their addresses and occupations, to Quarter Sessions. This requirement was abolished in 1967. Clerks of the Peace retained the certificates, and also kept registers of the Lodges from whom they received certificates.

Further Reading
• Lewis, Pat. *My Ancestor was a Freemason.* (3rd ed. Society of Genealogists Enterprises, 2005).

FRIENDLY SOCIETIES
Friendly societies offered the poor insurance for ill health, old age, widowhood, unemployment, funerals and other eventualities. Most were local societies, but a few were county-wide or even national.

Many societies were founded in the late eighteenth century. Rose's Act of 1793, in the hope that societies would reduce the burden on the poor rates, gave them statutory protection from embezzlement, misappropriation and theft, and made their officers answerable in law, provided their rules were approved by Justices. Not all societies sought approval; many were suspicious of government intentions.

After 1819 societies' rules had to conform with model rules drawn up by Justices. In 1846, the Registrar of Friendly Societies was established, and took over Justices' powers. Membership of societies peaked in the mid-nineteenth century, and rapidly declined after the National Insurance Act of 1911 inaugurated the Welfare State.

Rules made under the 1793 Act may survive amongst Quarter Sessions records. The new Registrar collected them on appointment in 1846; his collection is in The National Archives, in FS series. Some files include correspondence and member lists of dissolved societies. Registrar's reports were published in the Parliamentary papers series. Records kept by societies themselves survive infrequently, except in the case of national institutions such as the Oddfellows, www.oddfellows. co.uk/OnlineArchives, and the Foresters, www.aoforestersheritage.com.

Further Reading
The history of friendly societies is outlined in:
• Cordery, Simon. *British Friendly Societies, 1750-1914*. (Palgrave Macmillan, 2003).

See also:
• Gosden, P.H.J.H. *The Friendly Societies in England, 1815-1875*. (Manchester University Press, 1961).
• Fuller, Margaret D. *West Country Friendly Societies*. (University of Reading, 1964).

For a brief guide to records, see:
• Logan, Roger. *An Introduction to . . . Friendly Society Records*. (Federation of Family History Societies, 2000).

Records from a variety of sources, and from 755 societies, have been edited in:
• Morley, Shaun, ed. *Oxfordshire Friendly Societies 1750-1918*. (Oxfordshire Record Series 68, 2011).

GAOLS. *SEE* PRISONS

HOUSES OF CORRECTION

Houses of Correction were first erected in accordance with Acts of 1576 and 1598. The Vagabonds Act of 1609 required Justices to build them. In conception, they were intended to provide work for the unemployed. In practice, Justices found a multitude of uses for them. Unlike prisons, they were directly under their control. Disobedient servants and apprentices, the workshy and the mothers of illegitimate children could all be incarcerated. Houses of Correction became infirmaries for those with physical disabilities, places of restraint for those with mental illnesses, gaols for those suspected of felony or unable to pay fines. The vicious took priority over the needy, although the Richmond (Yorkshire) house in the 1620s actually paid inmates the statutory wage for their labour.[9]

Conditions were similar to those found in prisons, except that inmates were put to work. As early as 1630, the Book of Orders recommended that Houses of Correction should be built in close proximity to county gaols, so that the latter could share that advantage. West Kent Justices incorporated a house of correction into their new gaol in 1810.[10] Houses were supplied with tools, and with raw materials such as wool, hemp or flax. Salaried masters enforced strict work discipline. The relevance of separating Houses of Correction and prisons was increasingly questioned; they were merged in 1865.

Quarter Sessions order books include many orders relating to the fabric, staff and inmates of Houses of Correction. Bastardy orders commit parents to them. Eighteenth- and nineteenth-century records include the reports of keepers and visitors, accounts, rules and regulations, staff records and a variety of administrative papers.

Further Reading
- Van der Slice, Austin. 'Elizabethan Houses of Correction', *Journal of Criminal Law and Criminology* 27(1), 1936, pp.45 67.
- Innes, Joanna. 'Prisons for the Poor: English Bridewells, 1555-1800', in Snyder, F. and Hay, D. eds, *Labour, Law and Crime: An Historical Perspective*. (Routledge, 1987), pp.42–122.

LUNATIC ASYLUMS. *SEE* CHAPTER 8.

POLICE

Constables appointed by manorial court leets were responsible for medieval policing. If manorial courts ceased to meet, Justices made the appointment. By 1836, court leets were still appointing constables in 63 per cent of Petty Sessional divisions. Responsibility was transferred to Justices in 1842.

The duties of parish constables were many and various.[11] They collected rates and taxes, attended Quarter Sessions to present offenders, and helped to summon jurors (see Chapter 5). They raised the Militia and impressed soldiers (see Chapter 1).

An early policeman, sometimes referred to as a Peeler, after Sir Robert Peel, who founded the Metropolitan Police Force.

Parish constables were, however, unpaid, unprofessional and frequently ineffective. In 1839, the County Police Act permitted Quarter Sessions to replace them with new police forces. An 1859 Act required them to do so. In 1888, police forces became the joint responsibility of County Councils and Quarter Sessions.

The new forces acquired various non-policing duties. Some became inspectors of weights and measures, of nuisances, and of lodging-houses. Others kept order in court. Police licensed cabs and street vendors, controlled traffic, supervised the prevention of animal diseases, and, after 1870, school attendance. In 1862, Wiltshire police gave no less than 4,484 casual vagrants tickets for beds in lodging houses.[12] All of these duties involved bureaucracy, which led to the production of a wide range of records.

The early police forces are recorded in reports on the state of crime compiled by each chief constable, and submitted to HM Inspectorate of Constabularies under the 1859 Act. These reports (National Archives, HO 63), provide much useful information for the succeeding ten years. Other Home Office papers may also prove useful. The survival of early local police records is very patchy. Record offices and police museums may hold copies of the reports mentioned above, together with Police Committee minutes, reports, letters, accounts, and papers relating to police stations. Police records are primarily concerned with crime, and with the police themselves. Every policeman kept a notebook recording events that occurred during his beat, and every station kept an occurrence book. If these survive they can provide evidence of the commencement of police investigations. Charge books record names of persons charged, with details of their offences. Criminal and prison registers and photographs may give further details of convicts. Individual policemen are recorded in a variety of records. Attestation papers, constables' registers, discipline books, pension books and personal files may all yield details of individual policemen.

Further Reading
A good introduction to the history of policing is provided by:
• Emsley, Clive. *The English Police: a Political and Social History*. (2nd ed. Longman, 1996).

Nineteenth-century reforms are briefly reviewed in:
- Foster, David. *The Rural Constabulary Act 1839: National Legislation and the Problem of Enforcement*. (Bedford Square Press for the Standing Conference for Local History, 1982).

Police records are discussed extensively in:
- Shearman, Antony. *My Ancestor was a Policeman: How Can I Find Out More About Him?*. (Society of Genealogists Enterprises, 2000).

For a police history bibliography, a guide to archives, and various other resources, visit:
- International Centre for the History of Crime, Policing and Justice www.open.ac.uk/arts/research/policing/resources

PRISONS

County gaols were originally the responsibility of Sheriffs. They claimed costs from the Exchequer, and almost universally farmed out the office of gaoler. Gaolers held their position for life, regarded it as their private property, and, until 1730, could even sell their office. They received no salary, but imposed various exactions on prisoners, including charges for both admission and discharge. Most gaolers held alehouse licences and sold drink to their prisoners; for many, this was a major source of their income. Superior accommodation could be provided for prisoners able to pay. Gaolers could also collect fees from visitors. At Newgate, William Pitt, the keeper, made over £3000 from people wishing to see his Jacobite prisoners in 1716.[13] The arbitrary powers of gaolers, and their ability to determine their own prices for essentials, were amongst the worst evils of prison life. Many petitions to Quarter Sessions complained of gaolers' extortion.

Gaolers' prime concern was to ensure that prisoners did not escape and that court orders were complied with. They kept control over those aspects of prison life from which they profited, but were uninterested in exercising more general control. Gaolers' prisoners were their customers, and, indeed, sometimes their staff as well; they employed few wardens. Debtors might be segregated from felons, and men from women, but otherwise prisoners mixed with each other, hardened criminals with young offenders, giving prisons the reputation of being schools of vice. The hard labour sometimes found in Houses of Correction could not have been enforced in prisons.

A debtor in the Fleet Prison.

There were three broad categories of prisoners: those committed for trial or awaiting punishment, those unable to pay their fines, and debtors. Prisons emptied out when the courts sat: felons (see Chapter 5) were executed or transported, others (apart from the debtors) whipped or branded, and then discharged. Long-term imprisonment was rare before 1770, except for debtors.

Debtors frequently constituted more than 50 per cent of prisoners. Crown debtors had been liable to this sentence since 1178, private debtors since 1352. Imprisonment was not intended to punish them, but rather to secure their persons until debts were paid. Debtors' presence had an important impact on the tone of prisons. They mixed with felons, but could not be treated like them. They were always ready to complain of infringements of their rights as Englishmen. And they were one of the major sources of gaolers' livelihoods before the nineteenth century. Their plight was relieved by the Bankruptcy Act of

1861, which authorised registrars of the Court of Bankruptcy to determine whether debtors were genuinely insolvent; if they were, they could be adjudged bankrupt and released. Imprisonment for debt was ended in 1869.[14]

Poor prisoners were supposed to be supported by county rates under a 1572 Act. The allowance given was frequently insufficient, and sometimes many died when the price of grain rose sharply. However, some prisoners lived quite comfortably. They could carry on their usual trades in prison, if they could obtain the tools and materials needed. Others begged from barred prison windows.

Gaol conditions before the eighteenth century were appalling. They were insanitary, disease-ridden, overcrowded and notorious. Many lacked sewers, running water or facilities for exercise. Their inmates were sitting targets for diseases such as plague or typhoid. Death frequently prevented prisoners from being tried – and judges from trying them. At the 1586 'Black Assizes' in Exeter, prison fever – probably typhus – killed not just the judge, but also eight magistrates, eleven jurymen and many others.[15]

Security was also a serious problem, not always helped by prison buildings, which were rarely purpose built. Chains and leg irons were frequently used. But the need for security was frequently outweighed by the fact that gaolers could charge visitors fees, and therefore allowed them in with little supervision.

Some feeble attempts to improve conditions were made. The Gaols Act of 1531 authorised Justices of the Peace to levy rates for building gaols. It lapsed in 1582, but the Gaols Act of 1698 renewed the power. Little was done. Proposals to replace decaying buildings were frequently mired in the question of who was to pay. In Yorkshire, repeated presentments of the inadequacy of York Castle as a gaol between 1776 and 1821 led to no action until 1824.[16]

It was not until Sheriffs like John Howard used their positions to campaign for reform that conditions began to improve. Howard set out four reforming principles: prisons should be structurally secure and sanitary, should have reformatory regimes, and should be regularly inspected; gaolers should be paid by salaries rather than fees. The reform campaign coincided with an expanding prison population, as judges increasingly imposed sentences of imprisonment rather than corporal punishment or hanging.

Reform was gradual. The Penitentiary Act of 1779 was based on a penology requiring solitary confinement, a labour regime and religious instruction; it authorised the building of two model prisons. These were not in fact built, but many counties adopted the model after the Gaols Act of 1784 authorised the building of new prisons. A second wave of construction followed in the 1820s.

By the mid-nineteenth century, prisoners' lives were carefully regulated. Many undertook hard labour, most were subjected to solitude, and conversation and pleasure were outlawed. In 1823, the treadmill was introduced at Devizes Gaol.[17] The funds required came from county rates. Ratepayers, of course, objected to rate increases, and Justices generally sought to keep them down, practicing economy in every way possible. Even the urine of Wakefield prisoners was sold![18] It was used in blanket manufacture. When prisons were transferred to central control in 1877, one of the motives was to reduce local rates.

The office of gaoler gradually ceased to be a means of carrying on private business. In 1728, gaolers were required to post a schedule of fees. The sale of beer, liquor and tobacco in prisons was banned in 1784. Salaries began to be paid to gaolers: the gaoler at Horsham (Sussex) in 1779 was to be paid £100 per annum; he could not take fees or sell goods to inmates.[19] Newly-salaried governors saw their duties greatly enlarged. They already attended Quarter Sessions and Assizes, administered floggings and escorted prisoners to court (and to their ships if sentenced to transportation). They were now expected to give constant attendance, to exert strict discipline over both prisoners and staff, and to keep detailed records. Ensuring safe custody remained a top priority, but it ceased to be the only major priority.

The Gaol Fees Abolition Act of 1815 ended gaolers' ability to run prisons as private businesses. Quarter Sessions were required to pay their salaries. The Gaols Act of 1823 forbade gaolers to sell goods to prisoners, banned alcohol in prisons, required Quarter Sessions to appoint Justices as visitors and sought to implement Howard's four basic principles. Prison governors regularly attended Quarter Sessions to present their journals and registers of punishments, and the reports of the visiting justices.

A national prisons inspectorate was established by the Prisons Act of 1835, with a purely advisory role. It slowly cajoled the Justices into making improvements. Its reports, published in the *Parliamentary Papers* series, include digests of gaol returns. Inspectors' activities, and the requirements of reforming legislation, meant an increasing burden of expenditure. From 1846, the Treasury agreed to meet the cost of maintaining convicts. It was a short step from that to the removal of prisons from the jurisdiction of Quarter Sessions in 1877. Magistrates continued to serve as visitors, but their role was primarily to observe and advise.

Prisons generated much paperwork. Accounts, invoices, plans and letters record their building and maintenance. The reforms of the late eighteenth and early nineteenth centuries necessitated detailed book-keeping. By 1845, the governor of Ilford Prison (Essex) was able to list no less than twenty-five separate records he was required to keep.[20] The journals of governors, chaplains, matrons and surgeons provide detailed accounts of prison life. Registers of prisoners, punishment books and other records of prisoners, can be compared with the calendars of prisoners compiled for Quarter Sessions and Assizes. Prison admission and discharge registers for Dorset, 1782–1901, have been digitised by Ancestry www.ancestry.co.uk, which also hosts a digitised index to Bedfordshire prisoners, 1770–1882. The treatment of prisoners can be inferred from diet books and records of expenditure on their needs. Deaths in prison can be studied from gaolers' claims for burial expenses. Their accounts reveal the cost of escorting prisoners from gaols to Assize towns; the costs of escorting convicted transportees to their ships may also be documented. The National Archives PCOM series include much information on nineteenth-century prisons and prisoners.

Further Reading
An introduction to prison history is provided by:
• Morris, Norval, & Rothman, David J., eds. *The Oxford History of the Prison: the Practice of Punishment in Western Society*. (Oxford University Press, 1995).

For an older but still useful study, see:
• Webb, Sidney, & Webb, Beatrice. *English Prisons under Local Government*. (Reprinted ed. Frank Cass & Co., 1963). Originally published 1922.

Administrative matters are discussed in:
- McConville, Seán. *A History of English Prison Administration. Volume 1: 1750-1877.* (Routledge & Kegan Paul, 1981).

For prison architecture, see:
- Brodie, Alan, Croom, Jane, & Davies, James O. *English Prisons: an Architectural History.* (English Heritage, 2002).

All researchers should consult John Howard's work, which includes details of all English prisons in the 1770s:
- Howard, John. *The State of the Prisons in England and Wales . . .* (William Eyres, 1777). Various later editions.

A brief introduction to nineteenth-century prison registers is provided by:
- Hawkings, David T. 'Prison registers and prison hulk records', in Thompson, K.M., ed. *Short Guides to Records Second Series 25-48.* (Historical Association, 1997), pp.123–6.

The same author describes many convict records in:
- Hawkings, David T. *Criminal Ancestors: a Guide to Historical Criminal Records in England and Wales.* (Sutton Publishing, 1992).

PUBLIC UNDERTAKINGS
Acts of Parliament frequently gave compulsory purchase powers to undertakers of public works such as canals, railways, water and gas supplies, and other utilities, requiring them to deposit plans, maps and books of reference with Clerks of the Peace. Annual reports and accounts were also deposited. Turnpike trusts (see Chapter 13) are a particular example of such public undertakings.

ROADS
The Highways Act 1555 gave statutory force to the customary duty of the parish to maintain roads, creating the office of Highway Surveyor (or Waywarden).[21] Surveyors were initially chosen by churchwardens, constables and other parish notables, but, from 1691, by Justices from a list submitted by vestries. Surveyors presented the state of the roads every four months at Highway Sessions, and rendered their accounts to the Justices (vestries also saw them), who decided matters such as

road repairs, widening and closures. Any Justice at Quarter Sessions could present roads that needed repairs.

Everyone was required to undertake 'statute labour' on the roads, although this obligation was increasingly met by paying a fine; amounts were fixed by Acts of 1766 and 1773. By the beginning of the nineteenth century, statute labour was rarely demanded.

Surveyors could levy a highway rate under the 1691 Act. However, they disliked the odium of imposing rates on their neighbours, and preferred Justices to present, indict and fine their parishes for neglect of the roads. The fines imposed funded the requisite repairs.

Many documents relating to roads can be found in Quarter Sessions records. Presentments of repairs needed, and of roads obstructed or blocked, are frequent. There might be lists of parishes fined for neglect, naming surveyors and others, and indicating fines imposed. Sometimes local notables had to certify that the work had been done. Highway matters were frequently raised in letters from individual Justices.

Road management by parishes proved to be totally inadequate; turnpike trusts (see Chapter 13) took over responsibility for many roads in the eighteenth century. Nevertheless, parishes were reluctant to relinquish their control, hindering the implementation of the 1862 Act which permitted Quarter Sessions to create highway districts. It was not until the creation of rural sanitary authorities, under the Public Health Act of 1875, that responsibility for roads began to be removed from parish surveyors.

Much information on roads can be found in Quarter Sessions order books and rolls, as well as amongst parish records. Closures and route changes in particular generated much paper: they frequently led to petitions, the statements of local inhabitants, newspaper reports (especially in the nineteenth century), maps, plans, and orders, which are now invaluable sources for local historians.

Further Reading
• Webb, Sidney, & Webb, Beatrice. *The Story of the King's Highway*. (Frank Cass & Co., 1963). Originally published 1913.

SAVINGS BANKS
Acts of 1817 and 1828 required savings banks to deposit copies of their rules with Clerks of the Peace. Annuity societies were put under a

similar obligation in 1833. The Clerk of the Peace's certificate enabled them to invest in Treasury stock. These provisions were repealed in 1863. Copies of rules preserved amongst Quarter Sessions records may give the names of bank and society officers.

WAGES

Wage regulation in England began with the Statute of Labourers of 1351. The loss of perhaps a third of the population during the Black Death led to the scarcity of labourers, and consequent rapid wage inflation. The Statute limited wages to the level that they had been at before the plague. There were originally separate Justices of Labourers. In 1390, Justices of the Peace were given the authority to set wage rates for their own counties; assessment became a regular feature of Quarter Sessions procedures.

Wage rates for husbandmen, craftsmen and labourers were set annually under the Statute of Artificers of 1563. Justices were to consider 'the plenty or scarcity of the time'. Mostly, Benches continued the same rates for many years at a time; in Devon, an assessment made for spinners in 1679 was still in force as late as 1790.

Assessments were proclaimed in Hundred courts, posted on church doors, and publicised by constables. They were sometimes enforced; between 1607 and 1610, at least twenty-seven North Riding employers were prosecuted for paying excessive wages. Labourers seeking higher wages, or refusing to work for the legal wage, were also prosecuted.[22] In the West Riding, there was a 'general complaint of the inhabitants of these parts that servants refuse to work for reasonable wages' in 1641.[23] Enforcement was not always easy. Nor was it always attempted. Until the eighteenth century, the Wiltshire Sheriff's precept for summoning Quarter Sessions ordered him to return the names of those who had accepted wages higher than the Statute allowed. There is no evidence that he ever did so.[24] Wage assessments were kept by Clerks of the Peace, and may be filed separately, or with Sessions' rolls. Many presentments relating to non-compliance can be found, sometimes reflecting concerted action by Justices to reduce wages.

By the eighteenth century, the boot was on the other foot. Wage assessments set minimum wages, as well as the maximum. Workers occasionally demanded enforcement. There is little other evidence of prosecution in the later eighteenth century. Wage assessments gradually ceased to be issued; the last known re-issue of an assessment was made in the West Riding of Yorkshire in 1812.[25] The duty of Justices to fix wages was abolished in 1813, except in certain trades.

Further Reading
• Kelsall, R.K. *Wage Regulation under the Statute of Artificers*. (Methuen & Co., 1938).

WEIGHTS, MEASURES AND TRADING STANDARDS

Parishes had their own weights and measures, usually kept by parish constables. These were regularly checked against the King's standard at the county town. Quarter Sessions could take action against false weights. An Act of 1794/5 authorised them to appoint inspectors, who had to mark and seal all weights and measures. Various other Acts followed. Imperial units were established by the Uniformity of Weights and Measures Act of 1824, requiring copies of model standards deposited in the Exchequer to be purchased by counties.

Gradually, the powers of inspectors were widened. The Petroleum Act of 1871 gave them responsibility for licencing the sale of petrol; the Sale of Food and Drugs Act of 1875 empowered them to sample food and drugs for adulteration; the Explosives Act of 1875 regulated the storage of explosives for retail sale. Sometimes the duties of inspectors were carried out by the new police forces. Their duties today are carried out by trading standards inspectors.

The regulation of goods for sale was not entirely new. In earlier centuries, cloth searchers appointed by Justices had played a major role in the textile industry.[26] Searchers for defective tiles (from 1477) and pewter (from 1503) were similarly appointed.

Record offices may hold applications, testimonials and recommendations relating to the appointment of inspectors, returns of weights inspected, recognizances and lists of convictions. Registers of inspections list the businesses where weights and measures were checked. Registers of licences for storing petroleum had to be kept. Explosives' registers recorded premises where explosives were stored. Clerks of the Peace received quarterly reports from the public analyst on food and drugs under the 1875 Act.

Chapter 11

CORONERS' RECORDS

The office of coroner dates from the twelfth century. Coroners were elected by freeholders in the county court, or, sometimes, in the Eyre courts. It was not until 1888 that this method of appointment ceased in the counties; henceforward, coroners were appointed by county councils. Borough coroners were separately appointed, and will not be considered here.

Coroners theoretically served for entire counties, but in practice there were usually several coroners, each covering their own district. They held office for life. Before 1340, they had to be knights; after that date, the office could be held by any freeholder.

Originally, the coroner was *custos placitorum corone*, that is, the keeper of the pleas of the Crown. The title became *coronato*, and hence 'crowner' or 'coroner'. Their original purpose was to keep an eye on Sheriffs, who heard pleas in the county court, rather than to determine cases themselves. It was their records which had to be produced to the medieval Eyre courts, rather than those of the Sheriffs. Their absence in a county court rendered its exactions and outlawries null and void. However, their prime responsibility (at least since 1194), has been to hold inquests on unnatural, sudden and suspicious deaths, and on deaths in prison. Medieval coroners could arrest anyone suspected of homicide. They heard the confessions of felons who had fled to sanctuary and their abjurations of the realm; they investigated private appeals (accusations made against offenders) before trial in the Eyre courts, and promulgated outlawries; they investigated arson. Sometimes, the coroner could even hold the Sheriff's tourn. His rolls were frequently consulted by Eyre judges, who checked them against jurors' presentments.

Medieval coroners levied monetary penalties for the Crown. The revenue arising from the administration of justice helped motivate

An eighteenth-century coroner's inquest. (Courtesy of Welcome Images)

medieval kings to maintain law and order. The fine imposed by *lex murdrorum* (the law of murder) was the outstanding incentive for conducting inquests. Convicted felons and suicides forfeited their goods to the Crown: the coroner (with a jury) determined their extent and value. Deodands (the objects or instruments which caused accidental deaths) were also forfeit. Coroners fined the communities from which felons came.

Most surviving information concerning medieval coroners' activities is derived from rolls prepared for the use of Eyre judges, listing coroners' investigations. For example, in 1527, Thomas Goffe took sanctuary in the Chichester church of the Friars Preacher. He could only remain there for forty days, so he confessed to the coroner that he had 'assaulted Richard Barbor at Chichester with a knife worth 1d . . . giving him a wound of which he died'. He was required to go to Portsmouth by the most direct route, and to take ship, 'never to return without the king's licence and special forgiveness'. Goffe was probably one of the last felons to abjure the realm, although sanctuary was not officially abolished until 1624.[1] Whether he actually left the realm is another question; many abjurors simply left their own locality.

The county court originally provided coroners with their main sphere of activity. When it withered away (see Chapter 2), so did many medieval coronial functions. Private appeals ceased to be heard; sanctuary ceased to be offered; abjurations ceased to be made. The right to wreck was usually granted away to local lords, and thus yielded little income to the Crown, although it became more important in the seventeenth century. Deodands survived until 1846. In the medieval period their value had generally been low, but in 1838 a jury assessed the value of a steam boiler which had blown up at £1,500.[2] The coroner's prime role became the investigation of deaths and related activities.

Inquests were held with juries, summoned by Sheriffs or bailiffs, and sworn by the coroner. Most medieval jurors were local men; their numbers were variable. They were required to view bodies at the place of death. From the late eighteenth century, medical evidence became increasingly important; after 1816, reliance was frequently placed on autopsies.

Medieval coroners initially recorded their inquests on scraps of parchment, but compiled them into rolls when itinerant judges held courts; these rolls were subsequently filed amongst the records of King's Bench or another central court. The earliest (1128–1426) are in The National Archives, series JUST 1-3. Many have been published. These rolls ceased when the central courts ceased to itinerate, although the scraps of parchment continued to be used.

Coroners' inquests were frequently used as indictments for murder or manslaughter. They were not, however, conclusive in cases of homicide; there always had to be a trial before a definitive guilty verdict could be delivered. Inquests can be found amongst the records of Quarter Sessions and Assizes.

Numerous indictments are amongst the post-1554 Assize files. Indictment files from King's Bench (series KB 9, KB 11-14, and KB 140) include inquests relating to cases of homicide and murder after 1487. Writs *de Coronatore eligendo* (to elect coroners), endorsed with the names of those elected, can be found in C 24 for the period 1283–1633, and on the Close Rolls (C 54) until the fifteenth century. Coroners' records are also amongst the archives of various other Westminster courts, and of the Palatinate of Chester (CHS 18), the Duchy of Lancaster (DL46), and the Palatinate of Lancaster (PL 26/285).

After 1752, coroners filed their rolls with the Clerk of the Peace. There may be bundles of papers for each inquest held, including precepts to summons juries, depositions of witnesses and the inquest itself. The latter, following a standard formula, named the deceased (if possible), identified the finder(s) of the body, reported the circumstances and cause of death, valued the deodand and categorised the death as accidental, natural, etc. Any weapon used was described in detail. In the nineteenth century, printed forms were increasingly used.

From 1487, coroners could claim a fee of 13s 4d for each homicide, payable from the chattels of the slayer. From 1752, Quarter Sessions paid travelling expenses of £1 for every inquest held outside gaols, plus ninepence a mile for their journey home from viewing the body. Quarter Sessions order books may record payment of post-1752 fees. Bills may also be available; those for Wiltshire and East Sussex have been printed. They list all the inquests conducted since the previous bill, giving dates and places of inquests, the nature of each death, distances travelled by the coroner, and the fees claimed (which could, after 1837, include payments to constables, jurymen and medical witnesses). Coroners became salaried in 1860.

Nineteenth- and twentieth-century inquests were usually reported in local newspapers. They are increasingly available online; see, for example, the British Newspaper Archive www.britishnewspaperarchive. co.uk.

FURTHER READING
The history of the office of coroner is outlined in:
• Havard, J.D.J. *The Detection of Secret Homicide: A Study of the Medico-Legal System of Investigation of Sudden and Unexplained Deaths.* (Macmillan, 1960).

For the medieval period, see:
• Hunnisett, R.F. *The Medieval Coroner.* (Cambridge University Press, 1961).

For the period 1788–1829, see:
- Forbes, Thomas R. 'Crowner's quest', *Transactions of the American Philosophical Society* 68(1), 1978, pp.1–52.

Surviving records, with useful bibliographical information, are listed in:
- Gibson, Jeremy, & Rogers, Colin. *Coroners' Records in England and Wales*. (3rd ed. Family History Partnership, 2009).

See also:
- How to Look for Coroner's Inquests
www.nationalarchives.gov.uk/help-with-your-research/research-guides/coroners-inquests/
- Cole, Jean A., & Rogers, Colin D. 'Coroners' inquest records', in Thompson, K.M., ed. *Short Guides to Records Second Series 25-48*. (Historical Association, 1997), pp.114–17.

The reliability of medieval rolls as historical evidence is considered in:
- Hunnisett, R.F. 'The reliability of inquisitions as historical evidence', in Bullough, D.A., & Storey, R.L., eds. *The Study of Medieval Records: Essays in Honour of Kathleen Major*. (Clarendon Press, 1971), pp.206–35.

Eighteenth-century coroners' bills are considered in:
- Hunnisett, R.F. 'The importance of eighteenth-century coroners' bills', in Ives, E.W., & Manchester, A.H., eds. *Law, Litigants, and the Legal Profession*. (Royal Historical Society Studies in History 36, 1983), pp.126–39.

Some of the earliest coroners' rolls are edited in:
- Gross, Charles, ed. *Select Cases from the Coroners' Rolls, 1265-1431, with a Brief Account of the History of the Office of Coroner*. (Selden Society 8, 1894).

Local works consulted include:
Bedfordshire
- Hunnisett, R.F., ed. *Bedfordshire Coroners' Rolls*. (Publications of the Bedfordshire Historical Record Society 41, 1961). Covers 1265–1380.

Nottinghamshire
• Hunnisett, R.F., ed. *Calendar of Nottinghamshire Coroners' Inquests, 1485-1558*. (Thoroton Society Record Series 25, 1969).

Sussex
• Hunnisett, R.F. ed. *East Sussex Coroners' Records, 1688-1838*. (Sussex Record Society 89, 2005).
• Hunnisett, R.F. 'Sussex coroners in the Middle Ages', *Sussex Archaeological Collections* 95, 1957, pp.42–58; 96, 1958, pp.17–34; & 98, 1960, pp.44–70. Calendar of fourteenth-century cases.

Wiltshire
• Hunnisett, R.F. ed. *Wiltshire Coroners' Bills, 1752-1796*. (Wiltshire Record Society 36, 1981).

Yorkshire
• Barnard, Sylvia M. *Viewing the Breathless Corpse: Coroners and Inquests in Victorian Leeds*. (Words@Woodmere, 2001).

Chapter 12

ASSIZES

Twice a year, every county in England (except London, Middlesex, Cheshire, Durham and Lancashire) was visited by Assize judges. Between 1543 and 1830, the Court of Great Sessions performed a similar function in Wales.[1] Judges' names are listed by Cockburn for the period 1558–1714.[2] The judges served as the eyes and ears of the Crown, supervising the activities of Quarter Sessions, and adjudicating in difficult or serious cases. James I instructed his judges to:

> Remember that when you go your circuits, you go not only to punish and prevent offences, but you are to take care for the good government in general of the parts where you travel . . . you have charges to give to justices of peace, that they do their duties when you are absent, as well as present: take an account of them, and report their service to me at your return.[3]

The Westminster judges, drawn from the courts of King's Bench, Common Pleas and the Exchequer, sitting as the General Eyre, were first sent on circuit in the late twelfth century. The Eyre courts are outside of the scope of this book; for a general introduction to their records, see David Crook's *Records of the General Eyre* (HMSO, 1982).[4] Assizes succeeded the Eyre in the fourteenth century.

For the average litigant, the Assizes 'assumed the awful remoteness of a divine visitation'.[5] Hannah More likened the deity to an English judge, describing the Day of Judgment as the 'Grand Assizes or general gaol delivery'. More widely, the purpose of Assizes (and of the courts generally), before the eighteenth century, was not the pursuit of an abstract concept of justice, but rather the preservation of social order and harmony by a personal and judicious application of State coercion.

Winchester Great Hall, meeting place for Hampshire Assizes and Quarter Sessions.

The court was theatre, emphasising the majesty of the law, the awfulness of possible judgements, and the mercifulness of the judge. The law was intentionally harsh, so that its application could be mitigated by (variable) mercy. Judgement depended as much on the circumstances of the offender as with whether they had actually offended. Was the accused entitled to merciful treatment?

Attitudes changed in the late eighteenth century. Certainty of punishment began to be seen as the greatest deterrent; discretionary application of the law was regarded as weakening its effects. It was thought that punishments ought to be clearly defined, and less discretion allowed to the judges. Sentencing options changed too.

The local elite relied heavily on the Assize judges. Quarter Sessions referred to them all their difficult cases, and most felonies. The judges provided valuable legal advice, reinforced Justice's authority in setting rates, and provided an informal arbitration service. Assiduous Clerks of the Peace recorded their significant rulings in Quarter Sessions order

The Bloody Assizes. Judge Jeffreys denouncing the Monmouth rebels.

books, for future reference; many Justices of the Peace similarly recorded them in their own commonplace books.

Assizes judges were named in Commissions of the Peace, and sometimes sat as equals with Justices of the Peace. Their powers, however, were much wider. For example, they had authority over borough Quarter Sessions and over neighbouring counties, where others in the Commission could not adjudicate. Professional judges were first sent on Assize circuits in 1273. Fourteenth-century statutes gave them criminal jurisdiction, which they exercised until 1972, and supervisory powers over Sheriffs and other officers. As the powers of Justices of the Peace increased, so did the powers of Assize judges to supervise their activities.

Court administration was in the hands of Clerks of Assize, who were remunerated mainly by fees levied on litigants. Originally, they were probably the judges' private clerks. By the sixteenth century, Clerks had their own staff. These might include the bailiff, one or two clerks, the crier and the marshall. The latter two were appointed by the judges, and levied their own fees. The crier announced each stage of proceedings, the marshall kept order in court, and the bailiff brought the accused, together with prosecutor and witnesses, before the court. Clerks of Assize have been described as 'a compact and highly professional body'.[6] In *The office of the Clerk of Assize . . . together with the office of Clerk of the Peace* (1682) they had an extensive handbook for their work. Cockburn has listed clerks and associate clerks for the period 1558–1714.[7]

Assizes were held under Commissions issued by the Crown Office in Chancery. The Commission of Assize authorised judges to hear civil suits. The hearing of criminal case was authorised by a Commission of Oyer and Terminer, which also commissioned the Clerk of Assize and his associates and leading Justices of the Peace. The Commission of Gaol Delivery authorised the two judges, the Clerk of Assize and his associates, to try the prisoners committed to gaol. Clerks could act for absent judges. Until the sixteenth century, Chancery issued a writ of *venire facias* to the Sheriff, commanding him to 'produce' the Assize at a time and place to be notified by the judges' precept.

Before they left London, the judges attended Star Chamber to hear a charge from the monarch, or, more usually, the Lord Chancellor. Lord Burghley used his charge in 1598 to emphasise the importance of enclosure, depopulation, vagrancy and poor relief legislation passed by the 1597–8 Parliament. Within three weeks, Assize judges were urging local magistrates to implement these statutes.[8] Charles I urged on the judges the necessity of Ship Money in 1628, and the importance of the Book of Orders in 1630.[9] From the Crown's point of view, the prime task of Assize judges was to maintain communication with Quarter Sessions, and to ensure that local officers were acting in the interests of the Crown. Charges delivered to sixteenth and seventeenth century Assize judges, and repeated at Assizes, provide a useful guide to social, economic and political ills.

After the Restoration, charges were usually written. In the eighteenth century, the distinction between executive and judicial decisions began to be recognised; the judges became non-political, and were expected to use their own discretion. Their involvement in administrative matters became routine, and, eventually, defunct.[10] The perennial concerns of the Privy Council came to be expressed through printed questions issued to constables prior to Assizes. The former political role of Assize judges was taken over by the Lord Lieutenants. Nevertheless, in 1781 they were instructed to inquire into gaolers' abuses,[11] and they continued to oversee all important business conducted by Quarter Sessions.

Assize procedures began when judges issued precepts to Sheriffs, indicating dates and places for sittings. Sheriffs issued warrants to Hundred Bailiffs for jurors, appointed preachers for Assize sermons, and visited the judges in London (or sent their Under-sheriffs) to discuss the issues likely to arise, taking with them gaol calendars.

Hundred Bailiffs selected jurors, although Sheriffs could intervene. Twenty-four 'good and lawful men' were supposed to be impanelled, although the number was not adhered to strictly. From them, the jury could be selected. Jurors were not always impartial: in the sixteenth century, Harrison thought that 'certes it is a common practice . . . for the craftier or stronger side to procure and pack such a quest as he himself shall like of'.[12] It was not easy for his contemporaries to find sufficient jurymen; in Lambarde's Kent Grand Juries were largely made up of constables, whose attendance was compulsory.[13] Assizes used duplicates of the jury lists produced for Quarter Sessions.[14]

The verdicts of Assize Grand Juries came to be regarded as the decisive 'voice' of the county in political matters. When civil war was breaking out in 1642, it was before them that the rival causes sought approval. After the Restoration, membership acquired greater status; juries were frequently headed by baronets or knights, and consisted mainly of esquires, including many Justices. Such jurors could stand up to Assize judges when they had a mind to do so.

On arrival in the county, judges were met by the Sheriff's officers, conducted to their lodgings in the Assize town, and greeted by the county gentry. Proceedings began with the Assize sermon.[15] Some were long and pedantic, others caused a stir. In 1642, a Kentish Assize sermon led to the arrest of Justice Malet whilst he was sitting in court. He was escorted to the Tower.[16] Two centuries later, in 1833, John Keble[17] used his Assize sermon to launch the high church Oxford Movement.

The sermon concluded, the judges processed to the Court, and the clerk read the Commissions. The Sheriff returned his precept, putting in the writs of *nisi prius* which had been directed to him, plus the panel of grand jurors, the *nomina ministrorum* listing all those required to attend, and the gaol calendar listing prisoners for trial. The latter two were frequently written on a single sheet, although from the mid-eighteenth century printed calendars became increasingly common. The *nomina ministrorum* in the seventeenth century usually listed Justices of the Peace, coroners, and the bailiffs of Hundreds and Liberties: constables and borough mayors were generally not included. Absences were noted by a prick as it was called over. Many justices were usually absent – between 1558 and 1625, absenteeism averaged 52 per cent in the Home Circuit.[18] Death, illness, old age and absence on legal or Crown business were the usual excuses. Absentees could be fined, at judges' discretion.

Coroners put in their inquisitions, Justices of the Peace their examinations and informations, Hundred Constables their presentments (given to them by parish constables). The judges themselves brought documents from the Privy Council. Once the documentation had been placed before the court, the Grand Jury, consisting of between thirteen and twenty-three gentlemen, was called and sworn. And one of the judges delivered the charge.

The charge to the Grand Jury, like that at Quarter Sessions, directed them how to proceed, and what offences they should particularly inquire into. Its preamble included the instructions the judges had received in Star Chamber. Eighteenth-century charges became secular sermons, emphasising the blessedness of law and constitution, and the

152

virtues of authority and obedience. By this time, most Justices were well educated, and had little need for detailed instruction in the law, except in the case of new legislation.

CRIMINAL MATTERS

The Grand Jury responded to the charge by presenting the state of the county, and scrutinising the documentation. The court then divided into two. From the mid-sixteenth century, criminal cases were heard by one of the judges; civil cases by the other. Trial procedures were similar to those of Quarter Sessions. Grand jurors could make presentments of offences known to them personally. They reviewed indictments drawn up by the Clerk of Assize from the gaol calendars, or on the instruction of prosecutors. Clerks of the Peace forwarded indictments of *casus difficultatis* from Quarter Sessions. Coroners' inquisitions were treated as indictments in cases of homicide.

The Grand Jury, like its counterpart at Quarter Sessions, endorsed indictments either *billa vera* or *ignoramus*; the latter were mostly destroyed. Indictments might be amended to reduce the seriousness of crimes, thus mitigating sentences, or enabling the accused to make the fictional plea that they were clergy (see below).

Assizes were increasingly preoccupied with cases of burglary, robbery and grand larceny. Between 1558 and 1714, perhaps 70 per cent of all criminal indictments at Assizes were for larceny and related offences. Homicide indictments rarely occupied more than 10 per cent of the calendar. Indictments for witchcraft totalled perhaps 5 per cent, at least before 1680.[19]

Most cases heard before Assizes came from Quarter Sessions. Justices of the Peace preferred Assize judges to hear capital cases, although they did have the power to try them. Assizes increasingly heard appeals against Quarter Sessions' decisions, especially in settlement cases. Increasing business meant that speed was sometimes essential; as late as 1869, Baron Gurney was described as 'rushing through the [Assize] calendar like a wild elephant through a sugar plantation'.[20] Lack of time could force judges to refer cases back to Quarter Sessions. Cases could also be removed from Assizes to King's Bench by writ of *certiorari*. Relevant indictments, presentments, and convictions can be found in The National Archives, series KB 9 & 11.

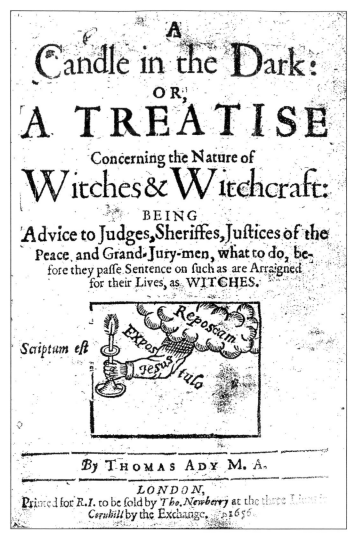

A Candle in the Dark *gave members of the judiciary advice on how to deal with 'witches'.*

Little is known about pre-nineteenth century trial procedures, except that they were 'nasty, brutish and essentially short'.[21] The nature of the evidence heard, the influence of judges, the outlook of jurors, and the extent to which the strictness of the law was tempered by mercy, are all difficult to assess. But courts were not dispassionate. The presumption of innocence until found guilty was not a doctrine known until c.1780, and not fully accepted until c.1820. Several cases were tried together, the accused being chained to each other. A petty jury was empanelled, indictments were read in the order they appeared on the gaol calendar, and the accused entered their pleas. The vast majority pleaded not guilty, and indictments were marked *po[nit] se*. Guilty pleas were discouraged; they meant the judge had no knowledge of circumstances, and was therefore forced to pass judgement without being able to recommend a reprieve.[22] Indictments of those pleading guilty were marked *cog[novit]*.

As at Quarter Sessions, prosecutions were mostly undertaken by the victims themselves, probably coordinated by Clerks of Assize. It was not until the 1720s and 1730s that prosecuting lawyers began to appear. The evidence presented in court consisted of the magistrate's written examination (although this was only read if it constituted evidence for the Crown), occasionally petitions or 'testimonials' from the locality, and oral testimony from victims and other witnesses. Confessions, and incriminations by accomplices, carried considerable evidential weight, as did the victim's evidence. Crown witnesses were called first; if they were poor, they might receive an *ex gratia* payment. Such assistance was not available for defence witnesses. In cases of felony, defence witnesses were heard, but not sworn.

The accused had to prove his innocence with very little preparation, frequently not knowing the nature of the evidence against him, and finding it difficult to summon defence witnesses whilst confined in gaol. The judge himself led the questioning of witnesses. Defence lawyers were not permitted until c.1730, but by 1800 they were frequently conducting more searching interrogations of prosecution witnesses. It was not until 1836 that statute permitted them to sum up the defence before the jury.

Most juries in earlier centuries probably spent little time on their deliberations, taking their lead from the judge. Judges could dispute their findings, require them to change their verdict or order a re-trial. A jury that refused to find as a judge directed might be bullied, fined and even imprisoned. Judicial intimidation was not ruled illegal until Bushell's 1670 case. William Bushell had been imprisoned when the jury he was a member of refused to find two Quakers guilty of holding an illegal 'conventicle'. He sued out a writ of *habeas corpus* to the Court of King's Bench, who ruled that, if a jury had to deliver a verdict as the judge dictated, there was no point in having a jury.[23] Despite the difficulties faced by the defence, many not guilty verdicts were pronounced. In the Home Circuit, they constituted 40 per cent of cases between 1558 and 1625.[24] Juries could also return a 'partial' verdict, reducing the gravity of the offence, and the punishment that could be inflicted.

Sentences on the guilty were passed at the close of the Assizes. Even those found not guilty could be punished by whipping or imprisonment, if the judge thought their behaviour warranted it. Otherwise, they were discharged, unless they failed to pay their fees. Before convicts were sentenced, they could make pleas in mitigation. Many claimed 'benefit of clergy'. This was a privilege originally granted to the church, allowing it to punish criminous clergy.[25] The church could not impose the death penalty, so felons sought to prove that they were clergy. In the medieval period, only clergy could read, so literacy became proof of entitlement to the benefit. Elton argues that benefit of clergy became 'an absurd moderator on the absurd savagery of the eighteenth century law'.[26]

To claim benefit, convicts were asked to read the 'neck' verse from the Bible (Psalm 51: 'O God, have mercy upon me, according to thine heartfelt mercifulness'). The illiterate could learn this by heart, so judges wanting to impose a severe punishment sometimes chose a different verse. From 1487, those not actually in orders could claim clergy only once. By 1706, many felonies had been made non-clergiable: murder, rape, poisoning, petty treason, sacrilege, witchcraft, burglary, theft from churches, pickpocketing and others. From that year, the benefit was automatically granted for all other offences; the reading test was abolished, although other offences were subsequently made non-clergiable, for example sheep stealing in 1741 and theft from the mails in 1765. Meanwhile, the obligation to turn clergied offenders over to the ecclesiastical courts had been ended in 1576. Felons were branded on the left thumb, or on the face between 1699 and 1706, and might be imprisoned for a year or two. Indictments were marked *legit* or *clericus*. Returns of those granted clergy were made to King's Bench between 1518 and 1660; a few of these are in The National Archives, series KB 9; many were abstracted on the controlment rolls 1558–1625 (KB 29/192-273). The plea of clergy was abolished in the 1820s.

The Artful Dodger by George Cruickshank, from Charles Dickens' Oliver Twist.

Women could not make the plea until 1624, and not equally with men until 1691. They could not be clergy. They could, however, claim 'benefit of belly', that is, plead pregnancy. Execution would be stayed until after the baby was delivered. Claimants were examined by twelve matrons to determine their genuineness. But delay was frequent, giving women an opportunity to become pregnant before examination! Women reprieved on this plea were frequently gaoled, although a few were executed after giving birth.

Capital punishment was only inflicted on a few. Juries were reluctant to convict if hanging was likely to be the sentence. Whilst judges could be harsh, most sought to avoid pronouncing death sentences, or recommended conditional pardons. In the eighteenth century, perhaps half of those condemned to death were pardoned and imprisoned, or transported to the colonies.[27] The purpose of the death sentence was to terrify, rather than to kill. It was valued for its supposed effect on those tempted to commit similar offences. Only a few hangings were needed to achieve that purpose.

Once Assizes were over, the Clerk of Assize endorsed the gaol calendar with the final disposition of the prisoners, and annotated indictments to indicate outcomes, in the same way that they were annotated at Quarter Sessions.[28] If a felon was unable to claim clergy, the sentence was the ominous *sus[pendatur]* (to be hanged), or perhaps *judic[ium]* (judgement). Juries returning a not guilty verdict following a coroner's inquest had to provide alternative explanations for the deaths, or accuse someone else. Fictitious names were frequently entered on indictments following coroners' inquests.

By the late seventeenth century judges were submitting a 'circuit pardon' or 'circuit letter' at the end of each session, listing those recommended for pardon. From 1728, they prepared separate lists of those they wanted transported or pardoned absolutely. Recommendations are in many National Archives ASSI and SP series. Criminal entry books in SP 44 contain many entries relating to eighteenth-century pardons. Crown entry books (or agenda books) for the South Eastern Circuit (ASSI 31), commencing in 1748, constitute the best source for reprieves and pardons for the area covered. Judges' reports on criminals (HO 47) between 1784 and 1830 contain detailed personal information.[29] This series also include witness statements, character references, memorials and petitions from friends and relatives of the accused (or from parishioners who would have to support his family on the poor rates). Judge's recommendations for mercy, 1816 to 1840, with lists of convicts, letters from prison governors, etc., are in series HO 6. Pardons themselves were entered on the Patent rolls, series C 66.[30]

Reprieve did not necessarily mean freedom; lesser punishments could be substituted. Convicts could be reprieved to serve in the armed forces. Branding, whipping and penal servitude with hard labour were

The prison hulk Discovery *at Deptford.*

common alternatives in the eighteenth century, although these began to be viewed with disfavour by the end of the century. Use of the pillory was abolished in 1837. For more serious offences, transportation and, subsequently, long-term imprisonment became increasingly common.

Transportation as a punishment was introduced in 1598, although little used before 1617. It was not until the Transportation Act of 1718 provided central funding for transportation from the metropolis that it became a major alternative to capital punishment. Contractors were initially paid £3 for each convict transported, and were able to sell the services of convicts to the highest bidder. Convicts transported are listed in Peter Coldham's *The Complete Book of Emigrants in Bondage 1614-1775* (Genealogical Publishing, 1998). Coldham's sources are described in his *Bonded Passengers to America* (Genealogical Publishing, 1983). Convict transportation registers for Dorset, 1724–91, have been digitised at http://search.ancestry.co.uk/search/db.aspx?dbid=2214.

American independence halted transportation. Many convicts were instead incarcerated in the notorious hulks moored in the Thames

A chain gain: convicts going to work in New South Wales.

Estuary, and expected to work in chain gangs along the river. Acts of 1776 and 1779 enabled judges to impose sentences of up to ten years in either hulks or Houses of Correction. These powers were used by the Assize judges much more than by Quarter Sessions, who had to pay the higher costs. Hulks provided an unsatisfactory means of punishment, expensive to run, and badly over-crowded. Mortality on board was high. Cook's discovery of Botany Bay provided a much-needed alternative: it enabled many convicts to be sent to Australia, which became a penal destination for three-quarters of a century.

Australian transportation registers, 1787–1870, are in The National Archives, series HO 11, and digitised at Convict Records of Australia www.convictrecords.com.au.[31] Many other relevant records have been microfilmed for the Australian Joint Copying Project www. nla.gov.au/microform-australian-joint-copying-project; the microfilm are available in major Australian research libraries, and its handbooks enable you to locate the original documents in England. A variety of other records are identified in 'Criminal Transportee' www. nationalarchives.gov.uk/help-with-your-research/research-guides/criminal-transportees, and 'Criminal Transportees: further Research' www.nationalarchives.gov.uk/help-with-your-research/research-guides/criminal-transportees-further-research/. Various county databases of transportees are listed at 'Convicts to Australia: a guide to researching your convict ancestors' http://members.iinet.net.au/ ~perthdps/convicts/ list.html

Even after transportation to Australia had commenced, hulks continued to be used. Prison hulk registers and letters, 1802–49, are in The National Archives, series HO 9, and have been digitised at http://search.ancestry.co.uk/search/db.aspx?dbid=1989. The nineteenth century witnessed the increasing use of long-term prison sentences; the purpose of sentencing gradually became to reform depraved minds through work, solitude and religious instruction, rather than to punish their bodies.

Richmond Bridge, Tasmania, built entirely by the labour of convict transportees.

CIVIL AND ADMINISTRATIVE MATTERS

Civil cases began before one of the Westminster courts, and were directed to Assizes by writs of *nisi prius* sent to the Sheriff. In early seventeenth-century Somerset there were perhaps seventy cases at each Assize. These cases required more care by the judges, as both sides were likely to be represented by counsel. Final judgement was reserved for the Westminster courts, to whom records of the proceedings – *posteas* – were sent.

Administrative matters, such as bridge and highway maintenance, rates, the erection of cottages and unlicensed alehouses, had to be dealt with by presentment and indictment. Many cases were referred back to Quarter Sessions or individual Justices. No less than ninety-nine of the 163 Somerset orders in the Western Circuit Assize order book for 1629–40 required considerable out of sessions labour for the local Justices.[32] Grand Jury presentments could be particularly important; in Interregnum Cheshire, the Jury criticised Justices of the Peace for allowing inadequate men to be appointed as constables, failing to hold regular monthly meetings in each Hundred, and neglecting to suppress alehouses. And they suggested candidates who would be suitable for appointment as Justices.[33]

CONCLUSION

An extraordinary range of topics came before Assize judges. Serious crime, the efficiency of local government, the regulation of enclosure, the oversight of economic projects, the maintenance of roads and bridges, the levying of taxation and relief of the poor, were all subject to their jurisdiction.

A more informal function of the Assize judges was to serve as the ears of the Council in the counties. Although the Council had many sources of information, none was as regular and reliable as the Assize circuit judges. They sat in court with the leading gentry, dined with them and were confided in by them; they judged their disputes. More formally, the petitions and presentments, examinations and informations they received allowed judges to assess the state of political opinion in their counties. Political allegiance and religious conformity were of prime concern to the Crown, at least in the sixteenth and seventeenth centuries. Judges were charged to report ill-affected, negligent, and feuding magistrates, who should be put out of the Commission – the ultimate sanction, which ensured that most Justices obeyed Crown directives. Sometimes, they urged action; for example, in 1629 the Norfolk Circuit judges reported that something needed to be done to revive the cloth trade in Bury St Edmunds, or it would fail altogether.[34]

THE RECORDS
Unfortunately, pre-nineteenth century Assize records have suffered badly. Assizes were seasonal and itinerant; they did not develop a tradition of record keeping. As early as 1325 they were ordered to submit their rolls to the Exchequer, but it is doubtful if this order, or the subsequent statute of 1335, was ever consistently obeyed,[35] at least until the nineteenth century. Clerks of Assize saw no point in keeping records not needed for current business.

The majority of surviving Assize records are in The National Archives, and particularly amongst the ASSI series. Survival from earlier than c.1800 is poor, although some earlier records have been printed (see below). Records from the fourteenth and fifteenth centuries are held in JUST 3 and other JUST series.

At the close of Assizes, the Clerk prepared three documents recording its decisions: order books, gaol books and *postea* books. Order books record a wide range of general decisions by the court. In 1736, presentments at the Western Assizes were recorded in a separate process book; orders relating to transportation also had a separate book.[36] Gaol books record convicts, noting plea, verdict and sentence. There may be separate series of minute books for particular offences, such as failure to repair roads and bridges.

The Clerks also returned their *posteas*, recording judges' findings in civil cases. These were the basis on which Westminster court made their judgements. *Postea* books were kept by the Clerks of Assize for their own records; these, together with minute books recording civil trials, can now be found amongst the ASSI series. *Posteas* returned to the Westminster courts are amongst records of the relevant courts. For example, King's Bench *posteas*, recording the initial proceedings, and endorsed with a record of the nisi prius proceedings at Assizes, are in KB20 for 1664–1829. Common Pleas *posteas* for 1573 to 1714 are in CP 36, and for 1830–52 in CP 42.

All the documents that came before the court were rolled up, perhaps using the *nomina ministrorum* or the gaol calendar as a wrapper.

Sometimes these are referred to as indictment files, although they may also include precepts, jury panels, coroners' inquests, recognizances, presentments, writs and other documents. Indictments were in Latin until 1733, except during the Interregnum. They appear to be a uniquely rich source of information on crime. However, the same strictures apply to Assize indictments as apply to those made at Quarter Sessions. They had to follow a set formula to be valid, but most give occupations as 'labourer', and most stated 'residences' are in fact the places where crimes were committed. Indictments and their related recognizances are frequently inconsistent. Medieval and early modern Assize indictments cannot safely be used as the basis for detailed economic and sociological investigation.[37] Nor can they be used to tell us much about actual crimes, as opposed to legal categories. Indictments for homicide, for example, usually accuse the defendant of murder, even though deaths were known to be accidental. When indictments began to be drawn up by prosecuting lawyers in the late eighteenth century, they perhaps became more accurate and elaborate.

Gaol calendars record the prisoners brought to court by gaolers. Sometimes they take the form of a book; gaol books for the Western Circuit, 1670–1824, are in ASSI 23. Early calendars name the accused, the offence, and the committing magistrate. From the mid-eighteenth century, they began to be printed, and the information given gradually increased; by the 1840s, Staffordshire calendars give prisoners' ages, literacy and states of health, with various other administrative details. Occupations and residences were added later in the century.[38]

Depositions (pre-trial statements of witnesses) tend to survive only in cases of murder and riot. Some from the seventeenth-century Northern circuit have been published (see below). Other records in ASSI on the criminal side include pleadings, coroners' inquisitions, jury lists, draft minutes of trials and administrative papers.

Assize and Quarter Sessions gaol records are not always distinct. For example, gaol calendars from the Devon Assizes were entered in Quarter Sessions order books between 1598 and 1640, and intermittently from 1646 to 1651.

Most county record offices hold some Assize records; for example, the earliest order book of Wiltshire Quarter Sessions includes many minutes of Assize proceedings. Related papers may also be found amongst the records of other central government courts and departments. Sheriffs' vouchers and cravings (E 389/241-57), detail payments for hanging, whipping and otherwise punishing Assize convicts between 1758 to 1832. Related payments to Sheriffs are recorded in T 53 (for 1676 to 1839), T 90/146-170 (for 1733 to 1822), and in T 207 (for 1823 onwards).

For the nineteenth century (1791–1892), the criminal registers (HO 27) record all indictable offences, including those tried at both Assizes and Quarter Sessions. Verdicts and sentences are noted, together with the dates of execution of persons sentence to death; sometimes they include personal information on prisoners. These registers can be searched at http://search.ancestry.co.uk/search/db.aspx?dbid=1590.

From 1868, gaolers were required to send both Assize judges, and Quarter Sessions, annual calendars of the prisoners they held. These include the following information: number; name; age; trade; previous convictions; name and address of committing magistrates; date of warrant; when received into custody; offence as charged in the commitment (includes name of victim before 1969); when tried; before whom tried; verdict of the jury; sentence or order of the court. Copies were sent to the Home Office, and are now in HO 140. Various other nineteenth century calendars of prisoners can be found in The National Archives, series PCOM 2.

The activities of Assize courts were of great interest to the general public. In Surrey, proceedings were regularly published commercially between at least 1678 and 1774. Gaol calendars and similar publications can be found for a few other counties. For London, the *Proceedings of the Old Bailey* (the capital's equivalent of both Assizes and Quarter Sessions) run from 1674 to 1913, and are available online at www.oldbaileyonline.org. Reports from all courts regularly appeared in newspapers; many can be found by searching the British Newspaper Archive www.britishnewspaperarchive.co.uk.

FURTHER READING
This chapter is heavily indebted to:
- Cockburn, J.S. *A History of English Assizes, 1558-1714.* (Cambridge University Press, 1972).
- Cockburn, J.S. *Calendar of Assize Records: Home Circuit Indictments, Elizabeth I and James I. Introduction.* (HMSO, 1985).

See also:
- Criminal Trials in the Assize Courts, 1559–1971
  www.nationalarchives.gov.uk/help-with-your-research/research-
  guides/criminal-trials-Assize-courts-1559-1971
- Criminal Trials in the Assize courts, 1559–1971: key to records
  www.nationalarchives.gov.uk/help-with-your-research/research-
  guides/criminal-trials-english-Assize-courts-1559-1971-key-to-rec
  ords

For civil trials, see:
- Civil trials in the English Assize Courts 1656–1971: key to records
  www.nationalarchives.gov.uk/help-with-your-research/research-
  guides/civil-trials-english-Assize-courts-1656-1971-key-to-records

There are a number of editions of sixteenth- and seventeenth-century
Assize records:
- Cockburn, J.S., ed. *Western Circuit Assize Orders, 1629-1648: a
  Calendar.* (Camden 4th series 17. Royal Historical Society, 1976).
- Raine, James, ed. *Depositions from the Castle of York, relating to offences
  committed in the Northern Counties in the seventeenth century.* (Surtees
  Society 40, 1861).

Cockburn has also edited many volumes of sixteenth- and seventeenth-
century indictments for Essex, Hertfordshire, Kent, Surrey, and Sussex;
for example:
- Cockburn, J.S., ed. *Calendar of Assize records: Essex indictments Elizabeth I.*
  (HMSO, 1978).

Other published Assize records include:

Gloucestershire
- Wyatt, Irene, ed. *Transportees from Gloucestershire to Australia, 1783-
  1842.* (Gloucestershire Record series 1. Bristol & Gloucestershire
  Archaeological Society, 1988). Based partially on gaol calendars.

Kent
- Knafla, Louis A., ed. *Kent at Law 1602: the County Jurisdiction: Assizes
  and Sessions of the Peace.* (HMSO, 1994).

Somerset

- Barnes, T.G., ed. *Somerset Assize Orders, 1629-1640*. (Somerset Record Society 65, 1959).
- Cockburn, J.S., ed. *Somerset Assize Orders, 1640-1659*. (Somerset Record Society 72, 1971).

Staffordshire

- Johnson, D.A. *Staffordshire Assize Calendars, 1842-1843*. (Collections for a History of Staffordshire 4th Series 15, 1992).

Chapter 13

OTHER LOCAL GOVERNMENT BODIES

Most Justices of the Peace also served on other Commissions. Some of these were temporary, such as those for disafforestation or for restraint of the grain trade. Others were permanent or semi-permanent bodies, such as the Commissioners for Sewers and the Parliamentary County Committees. In the nineteenth-century, Justices lost powers to various new bodies. Poor Law Unions, mentioned in Chapter 8, are an example. Boards of Health are another. All these bodies created records worthy of examination by local historians. Not all are considered here; departments of central government which employed local officers, such as escheators, excise officers, and ulnagers (who collected tax on wool) are excluded. So are the District Registrars who recorded births marriages and deaths.[1] Improvement Commissioners and School Boards were local rather than county bodies, and are therefore outside of the scope of this book. I have not dealt with forest courts, which were responsible directly to the Crown.

BOARDS OF HEALTH

Local Boards of Health were elected bodies established under the Public Health Act of 1848 and the Local Government Act of 1858, and played major roles in improving public health. In Salisbury, for example, the local Board spent £27,500 in 1853/4 on main drainage and water supply, leading to a steep fall in the death rate.[2]

Board of Health archives are likely to be in local record offices. Minutes, accounts, letters, personnel files and other records survive. Reports to the General Board of Health provide detailed descriptions of local sanitary condition, and present well-argued cases for implementing their recommendations. They are valuable sources of social and political history.

Further Reading
Reports to the General Board of Health have been published on microfilm. See:
• Pidduck, William. *Urban and Rural Social Conditions in Industrial Britain: the local reports to the General Board of Health, 1848-1857: a complete listing and guide to the Harvester Press microfilm collection.* (Harvester Press, 1978).

These reports are briefly introduced in:
• Smith, H.J. 'Local reports to the General Board of Health', in Munby, Lionel M., ed. *Short Guides to Records.* (Historical Association, 1972, separately paginated).

For other sanitary authorities, consult:
• How to Look for Records of Public Health and Epidemics in the 19th and 20th centuries
www.nationalarchives.gov.uk/help-with-your-research/research-guides/public-health-epidemics-19th-20th-centuries/

COMMISSIONERS FOR SEWERS
The word 'sewer' historically referred to artificial watercourses for drainage, rather than drains for carrying away malodorous waste. The earliest known Sewer Commissions date from the thirteenth century; they were ad hoc, granted to meet emergencies. Commissions were initially temporary, but many had in practice become permanent when statute law first took notice of them in 1427. Disastrous floods occurred in 1530; according to the Grey Friars Chronicle, 'this yere was gret wyndes and fluddes that dyde moohe harme'. This led to the 1531 Statute of Sewers, giving statutory authority for the granting of Commissions when need arose.

Commissioners' activities were administrative and judicial in character. They conducted surveys of the embankments, streams, and sewers in their jurisdictions, and had authority to repair them. They appointed bailiffs (sometimes known as dike reeves), surveyors, collectors, clerks, treasurers, and other officers. Rates were levied on landowners, who might alternatively be required to maintain their own banks and ditches. Commissioners worked closely with jurors, who sometimes held office for many years. Juries had to present deficiencies in flood defences before any work could be undertaken. Foremen of juries frequently managed day-to-day activities.

The 1531 Act only permitted Commissioners to maintain existing works. When new sea defences were needed, new Commissions had to be created by private Acts of Parliament. These lacked the judicial authority of older Commissions, which they gradually superseded. Surviving Commissions were abolished under the Land Drainage Act of 1930.

Many records were kept by Commissioners of Sewers, and by central government. Petitions for new Commissions are held by The National Archives, series C 191. Commissions were enrolled on the backs of the patent rolls (series C 66) until 1573. The 'laws and decrees' of Commissioners were approved in Chancery, and are in C 225 and C 226. After 1571, estreats of fines were sent to the Exchequer (E 137).

Records retained by Commissioners are now usually in local record offices. They include minutes of orders and proceedings, presentments (sometimes referred to as 'verdicts), reports from engineers and other officers, plans and petitions for new work, contracts with tradesmen, accounts, rate books and other financial records.

Commissioners of Sewers are well documented. Their archives present much evidence for a wide range of studies. Historians of the landscape, agriculture, and social structure can all find useful information, as can the genealogist.

Further Reading
The best general introduction to Commissioners of Sewer is Chapter 1 of:
- Webb, Sidney, & Webb, Beatrice. *Statutory Authorities for Special Purposes.* (Frank Cass & Co., 1963. Originally published Longman Green & Co., 1922).

For their records, see:
- Owen, A.E.B. 'Commissioners of Sewers', in Munby, Lionel M, ed. *Short Guides To Records.* (Historical Association, 1972, separately paginated).
- Owen, A.E.B. 'Land Drainage Authorities and their records', *Journal of the Society of Archivists*, 2(9), 1964, pp.417–23.

Lincolnshire
• Kirkus, A. Mary, & Owen, A.E.B., eds. *The Records of the Commissioners of Sewers in the Parts of Holland, 1547-1603*. (Lincoln Record Society 54, 63 & 71, 1959–77).

London
• Darlington, Ida, ed. 'The London Commissioners of Sewers and their records', *Journal of the Society of Archivists* 2(5), 1962, pp.196–210.

Norfolk
• Owen, A.E.B., ed. *The Records of a Commission of Sewers, for Wiggenhall, 1319-1324* [and] Owen, Dorothy M., ed. *William Asshebourne's Book*. (Norfolk Record Society Publications 48, 1981).

COMMISSIONERS FOR CHARITABLE USES
The Statute of Charitable Uses, 1601, tackled the misuse of charitable trusts. It gave the Court of Chancery authority to appoint Commissioners (with juries) to investigate complaints and correct abuses. Their decrees had to be confirmed in Chancery. Appointments of Commissioners, 1629–1803, are in The National Archives, series C 192/1. Inquisitions and decrees, c.1558–1820, are in C 93; depositions are in C 91; confirmations of decrees are in C 90; appeals against their decrees are in C 92.

COUNTY COMMITTEES
On the outbreak of the Civil War in 1642, Parliament created county committees to direct the local war effort. Committees developed from meetings of the Deputy Lieutenants. Various ordinances gave them power to raise money, impose taxation, and sequestrate delinquents (i.e. Royalists). Many judicial, military and taxing powers were granted under subsequent Parliamentary legislation. Some counties developed arrays of subordinate committees. Kent, for example, had twenty committees in all, including an accounts committee, a sequestration committee, and separate committees for each lathe.

Committee members were originally leading gentry believed to support Parliament. Most were Justices of the Peace. However, the lists of those nominated to serve were frequently 'optimistic anglings for support', rather than serious guides to the composition of Committees.[3] Those who did the work are best identified in committee order books and related papers. As the war, and the subsequent Interregnum regimes, developed, the elite gradually withdrew; committeemen were increasingly drawn from the lesser gentry and tradesmen. The county gentry were unwilling to impose punitive sanctions on neighbouring Royalists.

Many of the problems facing County Committees were dealt with in peacetime by Quarter Sessions. As already noted, some Quarter Sessions ceased to meet during the war. County Committees tried to fill the gap. For example, in Staffordshire, the Committee appointed parish constables itself; they were needed to enforce its orders. It also exercised jurisdiction over petty crime, and administered Stafford Gaol.

The major task of the Committees was military administration. They raised Parliamentary forces, providing the financial and material support needed. The relationship between Parliament, the Committee, local officers and the army command was ill defined, but the Committees were on the spot, kept a strict eye on the behaviour of Parliamentary troops and had a say in military strategy, although army officers did not necessarily obey their commands.

Committees acquired their own staff; the Staffordshire Committee had a clerk, a treasurer, and a number of 'commissaries' with specific responsibilities for hay, provisions, the magazine, etc. The Provost Marshall was one of their better-paid officials; he took substantial fees from the Royalists he imprisoned. Sub-committees had their own staff; each of the two Kentish accounts committees had a 'register', an accountant, a clerk, a messenger, a door-keeper and a treasurer.[4]

Finance was raised by the 'weekly pay', from loans advanced 'on the public faith', and from the confiscation of Royalist estates. Income from these levies was supposed to go to London, but, in practice, finance went to those who could enforce their demands. The local commanders who extracted money from the populace needed it immediately, and frequently kept it. It was sometimes dangerous to transport money to London. Nevertheless, the central Committee for Taking the Accounts of the Kingdom received accounts of what had been done; its records in The National Archives, series SP 28, are extensive.

Increasingly, County Committees became concerned with the sequestration of Royalist delinquents' estates. Their sub-committees seized estates and livestock, collected rents, felled timber, allowed maintenance to delinquents' wives and children and pursued defaulters. Accounts committees audited their accounts. Administration of sequestrated estates during wartime was difficult. Tenants suffered from the threat of Royalist raiding parties, and were difficult to find. Delinquents themselves frequently became the Committees' tenants. From their point of view, even if they had to pay heavily, they could at least prevent the extensive wasting of resources which occurred on some estates.

After the war, the difficulties of estate administration persuaded Parliament to allow delinquents to compound (pay a fine) to regain their lands. The Committee for Compounding appointed local sequestration committees, which sometimes merged with County Committees and their sub-committees. Sequestration activity, however, opened up the possibility of favouritism, prejudice, scandal and the abuse of power; it led to the committees becoming 'contemptible in the eyes of the Country' by 1647, especially when committeemen were of low status.[5]

Many County Committee papers can be found amongst the Commonwealth Exchequer papers in The National Archives, series SP 28. A few order books survive in the British Library and elsewhere; for example, the Staffordshire volume is now in the William Salt Library in Stafford. The papers of the Committee for Compounding are in The National Archives, series SP 23, and have been partially calendared.[6]

The Royalist equivalent to the county committees were the Commissioners of Array, or Arraymen. They similarly levied taxes and loans, sequestered their opponents' estates and provided local support to Royalist armies. However, they lost the war. Their records were incriminating evidence and were quickly destroyed. The only substantial record of Royalist county administration to survive is the order book of the Glamorganshire Arraymen, unaccountably preserved amongst the archives of the Diocese of Llandaff.[7]

Further Reading

A useful introduction to the work of county committees, with bibliographical notes, is provided in:

- Pennington, D.H., & Roots, I.A., eds. *The Committee at Stafford, 1643-1645*. (Collections for a History of Staffordshire 4th series 1, 1956).

See also:
- Mayo, C.H., ed. *The Minute Books of the Dorset Standing Committee 23rd September 1646 to 8th May 1650*. (William Pollard, 1902).

COUNTY COURTS

In 1847, a new system of county courts was created for the recovery of small debts and damages. These displaced the old county courts of the Sheriffs (although these formally continued to exist) and the various courts of request created during the eighteenth century. Both had only dealt with very small debts. The new courts received a huge amount of business: by the end of 1847, over 429,215 plaints had been issued.[8] They had no connection with Quarter Sessions; their district boundaries sometimes coincided with those of other local authorities, sometimes not. Judges were appointed by the Lord Chancellor, and appointed their own registrars and clerks.

The few surviving county court records are held in local record offices. Newspapers reported many of their judgements. Returns were published annually in the Parliamentary papers series between 1847/8 and 1858, and between 1867 and 1914–16. A central Registry of County Court Judgements was established in 1852; its registers are in The National Archives, series LCO 28. Useful information on other sources in The National Archives, and on related Parliamentary papers, are discussed in:
- Polden, Patrick. *A History of the County Court, 1846-1971.*
  (Cambridge University Press, 1999).

HIGHWAY BOARDS

These were created by Acts of 1862 and 1878. Quarter Sessions divided their counties into highway districts, in each of which roads were administered by a board consisting of parish Waywardens and the local Justices. Each board appointed its own clerk, treasurer, and surveyor. They took over parish responsibilities for the maintenance of roads, although individual parishes continued to be rated for the repair of their own roads until 1878. Boards also assumed the responsibilities of dissolved turnpike trusts (see below).

The establishment of highway boards was recorded in Quarter Sessions order books. Surviving records in local record offices may include minutes, accounts, reports, rate books, letters, plans, personnel records, and other papers. Their powers were surrendered to rural and urban district councils in 1894, although main roads became the responsibility of county councils in 1888.

TURNPIKE TRUSTS

The inability of parishes to adequately maintain highways led Parliament to create over 1,000 turnpike trusts in the eighteenth and nineteenth centuries, each by a separate Act.[9] The earliest Act was passed in 1662, but the next not until 1695. Promoters of trusts petitioned the House of Commons; their petitions, and Parliamentary proceedings related to them, provide much useful information. Trusts levied tolls on users, and applied revenues to road maintenance. Parishes might also have to contribute under the Highways Act of 1555, but that was rare. Local gentlemen, clergy, merchants and tradesmen, were appointed as trustees. Most Justices served on at least one trust; from 1823, they became trustees *ex officio*.

Trustees appointed clerks, treasurers, surveyors and toll keepers. These officers came from a variety of backgrounds. Clerks dealing with legal issues were frequently local solicitors. Treasurers were usually trustees themselves, and, increasingly in the early nineteenth-century, local bankers. Early surveyors came from a wide range of occupations, but were rarely competent in engineering. Their successors, however, such as Telford and McAdam, greatly advanced road construction technology. Officers sometimes held office in several trusts; the McAdam family collected no less than fifty-eight surveyorships between them.

Trusts installed turnpike gates and tollhouses, and set the tolls. The capital was frequently raised by mortgaging tolls. Trusts were created for terms of 21 years, but this was usually extended on petition to Parliament. Trustees, however, met infrequently. Attendance was usually low, and management often rested in the hands of officials. Many were incompetent. But trusts were independent, and not even required to render accounts. If they failed to adequately maintain roads, responsibility fell back on local parishes, who could be compelled to undertake repairs, although they had no remedy against the offending trust.

Justices of the Peace had some powers over trusts. They could arrange for roads to be surveyed, examine the applicability of tolls, determine disputes concerning funds, and check abuses. Travellers attempting to avoid paying tolls could be punished. Toll gates attracted much opposition from the poor, and were seen as an impediment to free trade. Receipts fell drastically when railways took over long-distance transport in the mid-nineteenth century. Trusts were gradually wound up towards the end of the nineteenth century and their responsibilities transferred to Highway Boards and subsequently to county councils.

Trust records frequently survive in local record offices. Minutes may record personnel matters, the leasing of toll gates, the evasion of tolls, the raising of finance, and the peculations of toll collectors. Mortgage books record the names of mortgagees. Other records include financial papers, surveyors' reports, maps, estimates, contracts for work undertaken, and copies of related Acts of Parliament. The latter can also be found in the Parliamentary Archives www.parliament.uk/business/publications/parliamentary-archives. From 1792, turnpike plans, and, from 1822, annual accounts, had to be deposited with Clerks of the Peace.

The records of trusts enable us to trace the involvement of local people, the techniques of road-making and the growth of traffic, as well as the history of trusts themselves. Family historians can use them to trace trustees, the staff they employed and the contractors who built roads.

Further Reading
For the history of turnpikes, see:
• Albert, William. *The Turnpike Road System in England, 1663-1840*. (Cambridge University Press, 1972).
• Pawson, E. *Transport and Economy: the Turnpike Roads of Eighteenth Century Britain*. (Academic Press, 1979).
• Webb, Sidney, & Webb, Beatrice. *Statutory Authorities for Special Purposes*. (Longmans, 1922. Reprinted Frank Cass & Co., 1963).

The records are briefly introduced in:
• Duckham, Baron F. 'Turnpike records', in Munby, Lionel M., ed. *Short Guides to Records*. (Historical Association, 1972, separately paginated).

For Parliamentary proceedings, see:
• Roads and Railways
www.parliament.uk/about/living-heritage/transformingsociety/transportcomms/roadsrail

NOTES

Introduction

1. Bates, E.H., ed. *Quarter Sessions Records for the County of Somerset, Vol.I. James I, 1607-1625*. (Somerset Record Society 23. 1907), p.li.
2. For a discussion of borough records, see West, John. *Town Records*. (Phillimore, 1983).

Chapter 1: Lord Lieutenants and the Militia

1. Murphy, W.P.D. ed. *The Earl of Hertford's Lieutenancy Papers, 1603-1612*. (Wiltshire Record Society 23, 1969), p.19.
2. Thomson, Gladys Scott. *Lords Lieutenants in the Sixteenth Century: a Study in Tudor Local Administration*. (Longmans Green & Co., 1923), pp.156–7.
3. Ibid, p.143.
4. Noble, T.C., ed. *The names of those persons who subscribed towards the defence of this country at the time of the Spanish Armada, 1588, and the amounts each contributed*. (Alfred Russell Smith, 1886).
5. Stater, Victor L. *Noble Government: the Stuart Lord Lieutenancy and the Transformation of English Politics*. (University of Georgia Press, 1994), pp.37–8.
6. For purveyance, see Woodworth, Allegra. 'Purveyance for the royal household in the reign of Queen Elizabeth', *Transactions of the American Philosophical Society*, new series 35, 1945, pp.1–89.
7. Murphy, W.P.D., ed. *The Earl of Hertford's Lieutenancy Papers, 1603-1612*. (Wiltshire Record Society 23, 1969), p.5.
8. Wake, J., ed. *The Montague Musters Book, 1602-1623*. (Northamptonshire Record Society Publications 7, 1935), p.l.
9. Listed by J.C. Sainty at 'Parliamentary Lieutenants of Counties (England & Wales)' www.history.ac.uk/publications/office/lieutenants-parl
10. For assessments made under these Acts, see Faraday, Michael, ed. *Herefordshire Militia Assessments 1663*. (Camden 4th series 10. Royal Historical Society, 1972), pp.29–185.
11. Stater, op cit, p.166. Returns to the questionnaires sent out by the Lord Lieutenants are printed in Duckett, George. *Penal Laws and*

Test Act: Questions Touching their Repeal propounded in 1687-8 by James II. (1883).

12. www.thegazette.co.uk/browse-publications. Official notices on a wide variety of topics are published in this journal.
13. Thomson, Gladys Scott. 'The Origin and Growth of the Office of Deputy-Lieutenant', *Transactions of the Royal Historical Society* 4th series 5, 1922, p.158.
14. For descriptions of armour and weapons, see Beauchamp, Peter C., ed. *The Oxfordshire Muster Rolls, 1539, 1542, 1569.* (Oxfordshire Record Society 60, 1996), pp.xxiv–xxvii.
15. Quoted by Boynton, Lindsay. *The Elizabethan Militia, 1558-1638.* (David & Charles, 1971), p.287.
16. See pp.46–7.
17. Boynton, op cit, pp.13–14, 91, & 220.
18. Carter, D.P. 'The exact Militia in Lancashire, 1635-1640', *Northern History* 11, 1976, p.89.
19. Thomson, *Lords Lieutenants*, op cit, p.86; Beier, A.L. *Masterless Men: the Vagrancy Problem in England 1560-1640.* (Methuen, 1987), pp.152–3.
20. Wolffe, Mary. *Gentry Leaders in Peace and War: the Gentry Governors of Devon in the Early Seventeenth Century.* (University of Exeter Press, 1997), p.143.
21. See the introductions to works listed at the end of this chapter for detailed discussion.
22. See the guide to state papers at www.nationalarchives.gov.uk/records/research-guides/state-papers-1547-1649.htm, and the guide to 'Militia' at www.nationalarchives. gov.uk/records/research-guides/armed-forces-1522-1914.htm
23. Dunn, Richard Minta, ed. *Norfolk Lieutenancy Journal, 1660-1676.* (Norfolk Record Society Publications 45, 1977), p.14.
24. See the TNA guide, 'Privy Council since 1386' http://www. nationalarchives.gov.uk/help-with-your-research/ research-guides/privy-council-since-1386/ For the published calendars, see Dasent, J.R., et al, eds. *Acts of the Privy Council of England, 1542-1631.* 45 vols. (1890–1964). These can be read online at British History Online www.britishhistory.ac.uk/catalogue.aspx? gid=156

25. Hatley, Victor A., ed. *Northamptonshire Militia Lists, 1777*. (Northamptonshire Record Society Publications 25, 1973), p.ix.
26. Ibid, p.xiv.
27. Beckett, Ian F.W., ed. *The Buckinghamshire Posse Comitatus 1798*. (Buckinghamshire Record Society 22, 1985).
28. Hopkins, Tony, ed. *Musters in Monmouthshire, 1539 and 1601-2*. (South Wales Record Society 21, 2009), pp.25–7.
29. Moir, Esther. *The Justice of the Peace*. (Penguin, 1969), p.144, quoting a letter from Sir Henry Bunbury to Lord John Russell.
30. Erickson, Arvel B. 'The cattle plague in England, 1865-1867', *Agricultural History* 25(2), 1961, p.102.
31. Hanham, H.J., ed. *The Nineteenth Century Constitution: Documents and Commentary*. (Cambridge University Press, 1969), p.403; Jebb, Miles. *The Lord-Lieutenants and their Deputies*. (Phillimore, 2007), p.94.

Chapter 2: Sheriffs

1. Garmonsway, G.N., ed. *The Anglo-Saxon Chronicle*. (Everyman's Library, 1953), pp.54–5. The place is identified in the *Annals of St Neots*.
2. On these, see Cam, Helen. *The Hundred and the Hundred Rolls: an Outline of Local Government in Medieval England*. (Methuen, 1930).
3. Gladwin, Irene. *The Sheriff: the Man and his Office*. (Victor Gollancz, 1974), p.183.
4. Cited by Peyton, S.A., ed. *Minutes of Proceedings in Quarter Sessions held for the Parts of Kesteven in the County of Lincoln, 1674-1695. Part 1*. (Lincoln Record Society 25, 1931), p.xvii.
5. Gladwin, op cit, p.281.
6. Noonkester, Myron C. 'Dissolution of the monasteries and the decline of the Sheriff', *Sixteenth Century Journal*, 23(4), 1992, pp.677–98.
7. Harrison, William. *The Description of England*, ed. Georges Edelen. (Cornell University Press, 1968), p.90.
8. Originally for military purposes, but under Charles I to raise money.
9. For the duties of Sheriffs during the mid-seventeenth century, see Mather, Jean. 'The Civil War Sheriff: his Person and Office', *Albion* 13(3), 1981, pp.242–61.
10. Escheators conducted *inquisitions post mortem*, valuing the estates of deceased tenants in chief.

11. Palmer, Robert C. *The County Courts of Medieval England, 1150-1350*. (Princeton University Press, 1982), pp.135, 229, 262 & 306.
12. Collett-White, James, ed. *How Bedfordshire Voted, 1685-1735: the evidence of local poll books, vol.1*. (Publications of the Bedfordshire Historical Record Society 85, 2006), p.xvi.
13. Palmer, op cit, p.43.
14. See p.83 for more detailed consideration.
15. Karraker, Cyrus Harreld. *The Seventeenth-Century Sheriff: a Comparative Study of the Sheriff in England and the Chesapeake Colonies, 1607-1689*. (University of North Carolina Press, 1930), p.19.
16. Ingram, M.J. 'Communities and courts; law and disorder in early 17th c Wiltshire', in Cockburn, J.S., ed. *Crime in England 1550-1800*. (Methuen, 1977), pp.123–4.
17. For some Staffordshire estreats, see Johnson, D.A., ed. 'A Staffordshire Quarter Sessions Fine Book, 1572', *Collections for a History of Staffordshire* 4th Series 16, 1994, pp.53–65.
18. Except in Cornwall, where the choice lay with the Duke of Cornwall.
19. www.historyofparliamentonline.org/volume/1604-1629/member/cholmley-sir-richard-1580-1631

Chapter 3: Justices of the Peace

1. Cited by Gretton, Mary Sturge, ed. *Oxfordshire Justices of the Peace in the Seventeenth Century*. (Oxfordshire Record Society 16, 1934), p.xcvii.
2. A detailed account of changes between the fourteenth and sixteenth century is given in Theodore F.T. Plucknett's introduction to Putnam, Bertha Haven, ed. *Proceedings before the Justices of the Peace in the Fourteenth and Fifteenth Centuries, Edward III to Richard III*. (Spottiswoode, Ballantyne & Co., 1938).
3. Moir, Esther. *The Justice of the Peace*. (Penguin, 1969), p.33.
4. Two early manuals are reprinted in Putnam, B.H. *Early Treatises on the Practice of the Justices of the Peace in the Fifteenth and Sixteenth Centuries*. (Oxford Studies in Social and Legal History 7, 1926).
5. For the forms of Commissions, see Skyrme, Sir Thomas. *History of the Justices of the Peace*. (3rd ed. Barry Rose, 1991), pp.1216–33.
6. Johnson, H.C., ed. *Wiltshire County Records: Minutes of Proceedings in Sessions, 1563 and 1574 to 1592*. (Wiltshire Archaeological and Natural History Society Records Branch 4, 1948), pp.viii–vix.

7. Smith, A. Hassall. *County and Court: Government and Politics in Norfolk, 1558-1603.* (Clarendon Press, 1974), p.72.
8. Sometimes known as the Lord Keeper, depending on whether he sat in the House of Commons or the House of Lords.
9. Harland, John, ed. *The Lancashire Lieutenancy under the Tudors and Stuarts.* (Chetham Society Old Series 49–50, 1859), p.xlvi.
10. Barnes, T.G. *Somerset 1625-1640: a County's Government during the Personal Rule.* (Harvard University Press, 1961), pp.44–5.
11. Smith, op cit, pp.32–3.
12. Ibid, p.70.
13. Coleby, Andrew M. *Central Government and the Localities: Hampshire 1649-1689.* (Cambridgeshire University Press, 1987), pp.23–4 & 102.
14. Webb, Sidney, & Webb, Beatrice. *English Local Government from the Revolution to the Municipal Corporations Act: the Parish and the County.* (Longmans Green & Co., 1906), pp.381–2.
15. Kimball, Elisabeth G., ed. *The Shropshire Peace Roll, 1400-1414.* (Salop County Council, 1959), p.29 &31.
16. Moir, *The Justice of the Peace*, op cit., pp.33–4.
17. Quoted by Beattie, J.M. *Crime and the Courts in England, 1660-1800.* (Clarendon Press, 1986), p.59.
18. Ibid, p.61. For recognizances, see pp.46–7.
19. Walker, Simon. *Political Culture in Late Medieval England: Essays.* (Manchester University Press, 2006), pp.94 & 101.
20. Johnson, H.C., ed. *Wiltshire County Records: Minutes of Proceedings in Sessions, 1563 and 1574 to 1592.* (Wiltshire Archaeological and Natural History Society Records Branch 4, 1949), pp.xii & xxi.
21. Skyrme, op cit, p.298.
22. Williams-Jones, Keith, ed. *A Calendar of the Merioneth Quarter Sessions Rolls. Vol.1. 1733-1765.* (Merioneth County Council, 1965), p.lvi.
23. Harbin, E.H. Bates, ed. *Quarter Sessions Records for the County of Somerset, vol. II. Charles I, 1625-1639.* (Somerset Record Society 24, 1908), p.xx.
24. Lander, J.R. *English Justices of the Peace, 1461-1509.* (Alan Sutton, 1989), p.39.
25. Moir, *The Justice of the Peace*, op cit., p.30.
26. Webb, op cit, pp.320–1.

27. Moir, Esther. *Local Government in Gloucestershire 1775-1800: a Study of Justices of the Peace.* (Bristol & Gloucestershire Archaeological Society Records Section 8, 1969), p.44. The 262 excluded honorary appointments.
28. Lander, op cit, p.38.
29. Webb, op cit, p.302.
30. Barnes, Thomas G., & Smith, A. Hassell. 'Justices of the Peace from 1558 to 1688: a revised list of sources', *Bulletin of the Institute of Historical Research* 32, 1959, p.223.
31. The minimal numbers of Justices 'not of the quorum' in the early eighteenth century is indicated in Skyrme, op cit, pp.419 & 1250–1.
32. Ibid, p.330 (note).
33. See p.115 below.
34 Crittall, Elizabeth, ed. *The Justicing Notebook of William Hunt, 1744-1749.* (Wiltshire Record Society 37, 1982), p.21.
35. Harland, John, ed. *The Lancashire Lieutenancy under the Tudors and Stuarts.* (Chetham Society Old Series 49–50, 1859), p.xlvi.
36. Webb, op cit, p.325.
37. Ibid, p.345, quoting Swift.
38. Skyrme, op cit, p.437.
39. Quoted by McClatchey, Diana. *Oxfordshire Clergy 1777-1869.* (Clarendon Press, 1960), p.178.
40. Zangerl, Carl H.E. 'The Social Composition of the County Magistracy in England and Wales, 1831-1887', *Journal of British Studies* 11(1), 1971, p.118.
41. Philip, David. 'The Black Country magistracy 1835-60', *Midland History* 3(3), 1976, pp.161–90. For the appointment of cotton manufacturers to the Bench in Lancashire, see Foster, D. 'Class and county government in early nineteenth century Lancashire', *Northern History* 9, 1974, pp.48–61.
42. Zangerl, op cit, p.123.
43. Cockburn, J.S. *A History of English Assizes, 1558-1714.* (Cambridge University Press, 1972), p.163.
44. Smith, op cit, pp.73–86.
45. Gleason, J.H. *The Justices of the Peace in England, 1558 to 1640: a later eirenarcha.* (Clarendon Press, 1969), p.80.
46. Phillips, J.R.S. *The Justices of the Peace in Wales and Monmouthshire, 1541 to 1689.* (University of Wales Press, 1975), p.ix.

Chapter 4: Justices of the Peace Out of Session

1. Crittall, Elizabeth, ed. *The Justicing Notebook of William Hunt, 1744-1749.* (Wiltshire Record Society 37, 1982), pp.6–7.
2. Morgan, Gwenda, & Rushton, Peter, eds. *The Justicing Notebook (1750-64) of Edmund Tew, Rector of Boldon.* (Surtees Society 205, 2000), pp.23–4.
3. Landau, Norma. *The Justices of the Peace, 1679-1760.* (University of California Press, 1984), pp.194–5, 206 & 208.
4. Sharp, Buchanan. *In Contempt of All Authority: Rural Artisans and Riot in the West of England, 1586-1660.* (University of California Press, 1980), pp.32–3.
5. Philip, David. 'The Black Country magistracy 1835-60', *Midland History* 3(3), 1976, p.181.
6. Forster, G.C.F., 'County government in Yorkshire during the Interregnum', *Northern History* 12, 1976, p.97.
7. Burn, cited by King, Peter. *Crime and Law in England, 1750-1840: Remaking Justice from the Margins.* (Cambridge University Press, 2006), p.20.
8. Beattie, J.M. *Crime and the Courts in England, 1660-1800.* (Clarendon Press, 1986), p.271.
9. Barnes, T.G. 'Examination before a Justice in the Seventeenth century', *Somerset & Dorset Notes & Queries* 27, 1955, p.40.
10. Oberwiteler, P. 'Crime and authority in eighteenth century England: law enforcement on the local level', *Historical Social Research* 15(2), 1990, p.17.
11. Quoted by Beattie, op cit., p.272.
12. For these changes, see ibid, pp.268–81.
13. For more detailed consideration, see Peyton, S.A., ed. *Minutes of Proceedings in Quarter Sessions held for the Parts of Kesteven in the County of Lincoln, 1674-1695. Part 1.* (Lincoln Record Society 25, 1931), pp.lxiv–lxix.
14. http://discovery.nationalarchives.gov.uk
15. These are analysed in Landau, op cit, pp.175 et seq.
16. Wiltshire & Swindon History Centre. Stourhead Archives 383/955.
17. Silverthorne, Elizabeth, ed. *The Deposition book of Richard Wyatt, J.P., 1767-1776.* (Surrey Record Society 30, 1978).

18. Davey, B.J., & Wheeler, R.C., eds. *The Country Justice and the Case of the Blackamoor's Head: the Practice of the Law in Lincolnshire, 1787-1838.* (Lincoln Record Society 102, 2012).
19. Morgan & Rushton, eds., op cit, pp.5 & 21.
20. Willis-Bund, J.W., ed. *Worcestershire County Records. Division 1: Documents relating to Quarter Sessions. Calendar of the Quarter Sessions papers Vol. 1. 1591-1643.* (Worcestershire Records and Charities Committee, 1900), pp.civ–cix.

Chapter 5: Quarter Sessions

1. Except in Middlesex, which also diverged from the norm in not holding Assizes.
2. Kimball, Elizabeth G., ed. *Oxfordshire Sessions of the Peace in the Reign of Richard II.* (Oxfordshire Record Society 53, 1983), p.37.
3. Moir, Esther. *The Justice of the Peace.* (Penguin, 1969), p.37.
4. Beattie, J.M. *Crime and the Courts in England, 1660-1800.* (Clarendon Press, 1986), p.149.
5. Forster, G.C.F. 'County government in Yorkshire during the Interregnum', *Northern History* 12, 1976, p.97.
6. Underdown, David. *Revel, Riot and Rebellion: Popular Politics and Culture in England, 1603-1660.* (Clarendon Press, 1985), p.265.
7. Hurstfield, Joel. 'County Government, 1630-1660', in Pugh, R.B., & Crittall, Elizabeth, eds. *A History of Wiltshire. Vol. V.* (Oxford University Press, 1957), p.107. See Chapter 14 for the Parliamentary county committees.
8. Burne, S.A.H., ed. *The Staffordshire Quarter Sessions Rolls, vol.III.1594-1597.* (Collections for the History of Staffordshire, 1936), p.xxviii.
9. For a more detailed discussion, see Devon Freeholders, 1711–99 www.foda.org.uk/freeholders/intro/introduction1.htm. Jury lists for Dorset, 1825–1921, and Surrey, 1696–1824 have been digitised by Ancestry www.ancestry.co.uk.
10. Quoted by Morrill, J.S. *The Cheshire Grand Jury 1625-1659: a Social and Administrative Study.* (Leicester University Dept. of English Local History occasional papers 3rd series 1, Leicester University Press, 1976), p.5. For jurors' attendance, see pp.9–12.

11. Webb, Sidney, & Webb, Beatrice. *English Local Government from the Revolution to the Municipal Corporations Act: the Parish and the County*. (Longmans Green & Co., 1906), pp.461–2.
12. Fowle, J.P.M., ed. *Wiltshire Quarter Sessions and Assizes, 1736*. (Wiltshire Archaeological & Natural History Society Records Branch 11, 1955), p.xxii.
13. Burne, S.A.H., ed. *The Staffordshire Quarter Sessions Rolls, vol.IV. 1598-1602*. (Collections for the History of Staffordshire, 1936), p.xxi.
14. Moir, Esther. *Local Government in Gloucestershire 1775-1800: a study of Justices of the Peace*. (Bristol & Gloucestershire Archaeological Society Records Section 8, 1969), p.99.
15. A detailed account of procedure in Merionethshire is given in Williams-Jones, Keith, ed. *A Calendar of the Merioneth Quarter Sessions Rolls, vol.1. 1733-65*. (Merioneth County Council, 1965), pp.xxxiii–xlvii.
16. See above, pp.38–9.
17. Jackson, Canon. 'Longleat Papers', *Wiltshire Archaeological and Natural History Magazine* 14, 1874, p.208.
18. Morrill, op cit, p.22. See also Leicester, Peter. *Charges to the Grand Jury at Quarter Sessions 1660-1677*, ed. Elizabeth M. Halcrow. (Chetham Society 5, 1953).
19. Landau, Norma. *The Justices of the Peace, 1679-1760*. (University of California Press, 1984), p.280.
20. Williams, W. Ogwen, ed. *Calendar of the Caernarvonshire Quarter Sessions records*. Vol.1. 1541-1558. (Caernarvonshire Historical Society, 1956), p.xci.
21. Smith, A. Hassell. *County and Court: Government and Politics in Norfolk, 1558-1603* .(Clarendon Press, 1974), pp.246–76.
22. Willis-Bund, J.W., ed. *Worcestershire County Records. Division 1: Documents relating to Quarter Sessions. Calendar of the Quarter Sessions Papers Vol. 1. 1591-1643*. (Worcestershire Records and Charities Committee, 1900), pp.ccxxxi–ccxxxii.
23. Moir, *The Justice of the Peace*, p.88.
24. Powell, Dorothy L., & Jenkinson, Hilary, eds. *Surrey Quarter Sessions Records: Order Book and Sessions Rolls, 1659-1661*. (Surrey Record Society 13, 1934), p.xxi.

25. On the cost of prosecution, see Beattie, J.M. *Crime and the Courts in England, 1660-1800*. (Clarendon Press, 1986), pp.41–8. Legislation of 1754 and 1778 did allow judges to award costs to poor witnesses who gave evidence for the prosecution.

26. Cockburn, J.S. *Calendar of Assize Records: Home Circuit Indictments, Elizabeth I and James I. Introduction*. (HMSO, 1985), p.89.

27. Beattie, op cit, pp.224–5.

28. Forster, G.C.F. 'The North Riding Justices and their sessions, 1603-1625', *Northern History* 10, 1975, p.121.

29. Kimball, Elizabeth G., ed. *Oxfordshire Sessions of the Peace in the Reign of Richard II*. (Oxfordshire Record Society 53, 1983), p.45.

30. Williams, op cit, p.lxv.

31. Ibid, pp.44–6.

32. King, Peter. *Crime and Law in England, 1750-1840: Remaking Justice from the Margins*. (Cambridge University Press, 2006), pp.308–38.

33. Hurstfield, Joel. 'County government, 1630-1660', in Pugh, R.B., & Crittall, Elizabeth, eds. *A History of Wiltshire. Vol. V*. (Oxford University Press, 1957), pp.101 & 103.

34. Lister, J., ed. *West Riding Sessions Records, Vol. II*. (Yorkshire Archaeological Society Record Series 54, 1915), pp.xli–xliii.

35. The book is printed in Kenyon, J.P. *The Stuart Constitution, 1603-1688: Documents and Commentary*. (Cambridge University Press, 1966), pp.497–501.

36. Webb, op cit, p.481.

37. Ward, W.R. 'County Government, c.1660-1835', in Pugh, R.B., & Crittall, Elizabeth, eds. *A History of Wiltshire. Vol. V*. (Oxford University Press, 1957), p.244.

38. For parish rates, see Raymond, Stuart A. *Tracing Your Ancestors' Parish Records: a Guide for Family and Local Historians*. (Pen & Sword, 2015), pp.54–5 & *passim*.

39. Forster, G.C.F. 'Government in provincial England under the later Stuarts', *Transactions of the Royal Historical Society* 5th series 33, 1983, p.38.

40. Willis-Bund, J.W., ed. *Worcestershire County Records. Division 1:*

Documents relating to Quarter Sessions. Calendar of the Quarter Sessions Papers Vol. 1. 1591-1643. (Worcestershire Records and Charities Committee, 1900), p.cliii.

41. Webb, op cit, pp.532–3.
42. Harrison, William. *The Description of England*, ed. Georges Edelen. (Cornell University Press, 1968), p.92.
43. Cam, Helen M. *The Hundred and the Hundred Rolls: an Outline of Local Government in Medieval England.* (Methuen, 1930), p.56.
44. On the confusions caused to historians by the development of Petty Sessions, see Gretton, Mary Sturge, ed. *Oxfordshire Justices of the Peace in the Seventeenth Century.* (Oxfordshire Record Society 16, 1934), pp.lxxxi–lxxxiv.
45. Willis-Bund, op cit, p.xxxi.
46. Gretton, Mary Sturge, ed. *Oxfordshire Justices of the Peace in the seventeenth century.* (Oxfordshire Record Society, 16, 1934), p.lvxxxiv.
47. Landau, op cit, pp.209 & 228–32. See p.83 below for clerks.
48. See p.24.
49. See pp.113–14.
50. For a detailed account of the construction of such rolls, see Jeaffreson, John Cordy, ed. *Middlesex County Records, vol.1.* (Middlesex County Record Society, 1886), pp.xxvii–xxix.
51. Those for Gloucestershire are included in Wyatt, Irene, ed. *Transportees from Gloucestershire to Australia, 1783-1842.* (Gloucestershire Record Series 1, Bristol & Gloucestershire Archaeological Society, 1988). They supplement the convict transportation registers, now in The National Archives HO 11.
52. See, for example, Beattie, op cit. He outlines the problems with indentures on pp.19–21.
53. Quoted by Willis-Bund, op cit, pp.vi–vii.
54. Petty Sessional records for Hackney have been printed; see Paley, R. ed. *Justice in Eighteenth Century Hackney: the Justicing Notebook of Henry Norris and the Hackney Petty Sessions Book.* (London Record Society Publications, 28, 1991).
55. For late nineteenth and twentieth-century Petty Sessions records, see Flynn, Sarah, & Stevens, Mark. 'Petty criminals,

publicans and sinners: Petty Sessions records in the Berkshire Record Office', *Journal of the Society of Archivists* 16(1), 1995, pp.41–53.

Chapter 6: The Clerk of the Peace and Other Officers
1. Fowle, J.P.M., ed. *Wiltshire Quarter Sessions and Assizes, 1736.* (Wiltshire Archaeological & Natural History Society Records Branch 11, 1955), p.xi.
2. See www.histpop.org
3. Bacon, cited by Peyton, S.A., ed. *Minutes of Proceedings in Quarter Sessions held for the Parts of Kesteven in the County of Lincoln, 1674-1695. Part 1.* (Lincoln Record Society 25, 1931), p.xl.
4. Morrill, J.S. *The Cheshire Grand Jury, 1625-1659: a Social and Administrative Study.* (Leicester University Press, 1976), p.59.
5. Webb, Sidney, & Webb, Beatrice. *English Local Government from the Revolution to the Municipal Corporations Act: the Parish and the County.* (Longmans Green & Co., 1906), p.496.
6. Ibid, p.497.
7. Ibid, pp.501–2.
8. Fraser, C.M., ed. *Durham Quarter Sessions Rolls, 1471-1625.* (Surtees Society 198, 1991), p.12.
9. For a detailed discussion, see Raymond, Stuart A. *Tracing Your Ancestors' Parish Records.* (Pen & Sword, 2015), passim. For highway surveyors, see pp.137–8 below.
10. Moir, Esther. *The Justice of the Peace.* (Penguin, 1969), p.117.

Chapter 7: Trades and Occupations
1. Willis-Bund, J.W., ed. *Worcestershire County Records. Division 1: Documents relating to Quarter Sessions. Calendar of the Quarter Sessions papers Vol. 1. 1591-1643.* (Worcestershire Records and Charities Committee, 1900), p.xiii.
2. Ibid, p.clxix.
3. Barnes, T.G. *Somerset 1625-1640: a County's Government during the Personal Rule.* (Harvard University Press, 1961), p.65.
4. Ibid, p.55.
5. Cockburn, J.S. 'The North Riding justices, 1690-1750: a study in

local administration', *Yorkshire Archaeological Journal*, 41(3), 1962, p.489.

6. Webb, Sidney, & Webb, Beatrice. *English Local Government from the Revolution to the Municipal Corporations Act: the Parish and the County.* (Longmans Green & Co., 1906), p.523.

7. See below, p.121.

8. Taverner, R.L. 'The administrative work of the Devon justices in the 17th century', *Devonshire Association ... Report & Transactions*, 100, 1968, p.80.

9. Barnes, op cit, p.66.

10. The requirement for testimonials had lapsed by 1660; cf. Kelsall, R.K. *Wage Regulation under the Statute of Artificers.* (Methuen & Co., 1938), p.40.

11. Forster, G.C.F. 'The North Riding Justices and their sessions, 1603-1625', *Northern History* 10, 1975, pp.120–1; Philip, David. 'The Black Country magistracy 1835-60', *Midland History* 3(3), 1976, p.180.

12. Kelsall, op cit, p.58.

Chapter 8: Paupers, Vagrants and Lunatics

1. See Raymond, Stuart A. *Tracing Your Ancestors' Parish Records: a Guide for Family and Local Historians.* (Pen & Sword, 2015), for a detailed discussion.

2. Ward, W.R. 'County government since 1835', in Pugh, R.B., & Crittall, Elizabeth, eds. *A History of Wiltshire, vol.V.* (Oxford University Press, 1955), p.253.

3. Wake, Joan, ed. *Quarter Sessions Records of the County of Northampton. Files for 6 Charles I and Commonwealth (A.D. 1630, 1657, 1657-8).* (Northamptonshire Record Society Publications 1, 1924), p.xxvi.

4. Cockburn, J.S. 'The North Riding justices, 1690-1750: a study in local administration', *Yorkshire Archaeological Journal*, 41(3), 1962, p.508.

5. Morgan, Gwenda, & Rushton, Peter, eds. *The Justicing Notebook (1750-64) of Edmund Tew, Rector of Boldon.* (Surtees Society 205, 2000).

6. Beier, A.L. *Masterless Men: the Vagrancy Problem in England 1560-1642.* (Methuen, 1985), pp.15 & 47.

7. Bartlett, Peter. *The Poor Law of Lunacy: the Administration of Pauper Lunatics in Mid-nineteenth-century England.* (Leicester University Press, 1999), pp.35 & 60. The 1807 figures do not include criminal lunatics.
8. Ibid, pp.154 & 191 (note 16)
9. Abstracted in 'Index of English and Welsh Lunatic Asylums and Mental Hospitals' www.studymore.org.uk/4_13_ta.htm
10. For details, see Bartlett, op cit, pp.162–72 & 278–9.

Chapter 9: Religion
1. Bunyan, John. *Grace Abounding & the Life and Death of Mr Badman.* (Everyman's Library, 1928), pp.103–29.
2. For a detailed guide to law and procedure, see Bowler, Hugh, ed. *Recusant Roll No.2 (1593-1594).* (Catholic Record Society 57, 1965), pp.vii–xliii.
3. Thomson, Gladys Scott. *Lords Lieutenants in the Sixteenth Century: a Study in Tudor Local Administration.* (Longmans Green & Co., 1923), p.136.
4. Shorrocks, Derek, ed. *Bishop Still's Visitation 1594, and the 'smale boooke' of the Clerk of the Peace for Somerset, 1593-5.* (Somerset Record Society 84, 1998), pp.132 & 170.
5. Wake, J., ed. *The Montague Musters Book, 1602-1623.* (Northamptonshire Record Society 7, 1935), p.xlii.
6. Forster, G.C.F. 'County government in Yorkshire during the Interregnum', *Northern History* 12, 1976, p.97.
7. Racaut, L. 'The book of sports and Sabbatarian legislation in Lancashire, 1579-1616', *Northern History* 33, 1997, p.75.
8. Tait, James, ed. *Lancashire Quarter Sessions records. Vol.1. Quarter Sessions rolls, 1590-1606.* (Chetham Society, New Series 77, 1917), p.xvii.
9. For Exchequer procedure, see Bowler, Hugh, ed. *Recusant Roll No.2 (1593-1594).* (Catholic Record Society 57, 1965), pp.lviii–lxviii.
10. For a detailed analysis of their content, see ibid, pp.lxviii–cix.
11. Jarvis, Rupert C. *The Jacobite Risings of 1715 and 1745.* (Record series 1. Cumberland County Council, 1954), p.10.

12. Printed in part by Kenyon, J.P., ed. *The Stuart Constitution: Documents and Commentary.* (Cambridge University Press, 1966), pp.461–2.
13. Landau, Norma. *The Justices of the Peace, 1679-1760.* (University of California Press, 1984), p.71.
14. 'Loyalists of Babington Hundred, 1660', *Notes & Queries for Somerset & Dorset* 24, 1943–6, pp.134–5.
15. Vallance, Edward. 'The 1723 oath rolls in England: an electronic finding list'. www.historyworkingpapers.org/?page_id=373#_ftn5. See also Dibbs, Sylvia J. 'The loyalty oaths rolls of 1723: an early census', *Genealogists' Magazine* 31(6), 2014, pp.225–9.
16. But see Gibson, Jeremy, & Dell, Alan. *The Protestation Returns 1641-42, and Other Contemporary Listings.* (Federation of Family History Societies, 1994).
17. For civil marriage during the Interregnum, see p.44 above.
18. *Parliamentary Papers* 1830, XIX (664).

Chapter 10: The Court as Administrator and Supervisor

1. For a detailed discussion of their work, see Chalklin, Christopher. *English Counties and Public Buildings, 1650-1830.* (Hambledon Press, 1998), pp.67–91.
2. Albert, William. *The Turnpike Road System in England, 1663-1840.* (Cambridge University Press, 1972), pp.168–87.
3. Raymond, Stuart A. *Tracing Your Ancestors' Parish Records.* (Pen & Sword, 2015), pp.160–3.
4. Peyton, S.A., ed. *Minutes of Proceedings in Quarter Sessions held for the Parts of Kesteven in the County of Lincoln, 1674-1695. Part 1.* (Lincoln Record Society 25, 1931), pp.ci–cii.
5. Hearing, Terry, & Bridges, Sarah, eds. *Dorset Quarter Sessions Order Book, 1625-1638: a Calendar.* (Dorset Record Society 14, 2006), p.x.
6. Essex Record Office Q/AMm 1/1-2.
7. Emmison, F.G. *Guide to the Essex Record Office.* (2nd ed. Essex County Council, 1969), p.14.
8. For alternatives, see Wormleighton, Tim. *Title Deeds for Family Historians.* (Family History Partnership, 2012).

9. McConville, Seán. *A History of English Prison Administration. Volume 1: 1750-1877.* (Routledge & Kegan Paul, 1981), p.45.

10. Chalklin, C.W., ed. *New Maidstone Gaol Order Book, 1805-1823.* (Kent Archaeological Society Records 23, 1984), p.15.

11. A detailed account is given by Kent, Joan R. *The English Village Constable 1598-1642: a Social and Administrative Study.* (Clarendon Press, 1986). See also Raymond, op cit, pp.27–30 & 77–85.

12. Ward, W.R. 'County government, c.1660-1835', in Pugh, R.B., & Crittall, Elizabeth, eds. *A History of Wiltshire. Vol. V.* (Oxford University Press, 1957), p.244.

13. Brodie, Alan, Croom, Jane, & Davies, James O. *English Prisons: an Architectural History.* (English Heritage, 2002), p.10.

14. For information on bankruptcy records, visit the National Archives page on 'Bankrupts and Insolvent Debtors' www.nationalarchives.gov.uk/help-with-your-research/research-guides/bankrupts-insolvent-debtors/

15. Taverner, R.L. 'The administrative work of the Devon justices in the 17th century', *Devonshire Association … report & transactions* 100, 1968, p.58.

16. Peacock, A.E. 'The creation of the West Riding Court of Assize', *Northern History* 23, 1987, p.121.

17. Ward, W.R. 'County government, c.1660-1835', in Pugh, R.B., & Crittall, Elizabeth, eds. *A History of Wiltshire. Vol. V.* (Oxford University Press, 1957), p.188.

18. Harrison, J.F. 'The Justices and the Prison Act, 1877: the example of Wakefield', *Northern History* 39(2), 2002, p.250.

19. McConville, op cit, p.90.

20. Ibid, p.278.

21. For Highway Surveyors, see Raymond, op cit, pp.30–1 & 76–7.

22. Forster, G.C.F. 'The North Riding Justices and their sessions, 1603-1625', *Northern History* 10, 1975, p.120. But see Kelsall, R.K. *Wage Regulation under the Statute of Artificers.* (Methuen & Co., 1938), pp.16–20 for a discussion of the frequency of enforcement.

23. Lister, J., ed. *West Riding Sessions Records, vol.II.* (Yorkshire Archaeological Society Record Series 54, 1915), p.xxxviii.
24. Fowle, J.P.M., ed. *Wiltshire Quarter Sessions and Assizes, 1736.* (Wiltshire Archaeological & Natural History Society Records Branch 11, 1955), p.xix.
25. Kelsall, op cit, p.103.
26. For searchers in Gloucestershire, see Willcox, William Bradford. *Gloucestershire: a Study in Local Government 1590-1640.* (Yale University Press, 1940), pp.164–71.

Chapter 11: Coroners' Records
1. Hunnisett, R.F. 'The last Sussex abjurations', *Sussex Archaeological Collections* 102, 1964, pp.44 & 46–7.
2. Forbes, Thomas R. 'Crowner's quest', *Transactions of the American Philosophical Society* 68(1), 1978, p.7.

Chapter 12: Assizes
1. See Parry, Glyn. *A Guide to the Records of the Court of Great Sessions.* (National Library of Wales, 1995). The National Library of Wales's Crime and Punishment database www.llgc.org.uk/sesiwn_fawr/index_s.htm lists criminals tried before the court.
2. Cockburn, J.S. *A History of English Assizes, 1558-1714.* (Cambridge University Press, 1972), pp.262–93.
3. Ibid, p.10.
4. For a briefer introduction, see 'General eyres 1194-1348' www.nationalarchives.gov.uk/help-with-your-research-guides/general-eyres-1194-1348.htm
5. Cockburn, *English Assizes*, op cit, p.3.
6. For a brief discussion of their work, see Cockburn, J.S. *Calendar of Assize Records: Home Circuit Indictments, Elizabeth I and James I. Introduction.* (HMSO, 1985), pp.2 & 4–10.
7. Cockburn, *English Assizes*, op cit, pp.314–21.
8. Ibid, pp.182–3.
9. Barnes, T.G. 'A charge to the judges of Assize, 1627/8', *Huntington Library Quarterly* 24(3), 1961, pp.251–6. See also p.67.

10. Cockburn, *English Assizes*, op cit, p.187; Landau, Norma. *The Justices of the Peace, 1679-1760.* (University of California Press, 1984), p.7.

11. Moir, Esther. *Local Government in Gloucestershire 1775-1800: a study of Justices of the Peace.* (Bristol & Gloucestershire Archaeological Society Records Section 8, 1969), p.141

12. Harrison, William. *The Description of England*, ed. Georges Edelen. (Cornell University Press, 1968), p.91.

13. Cited by Cockburn. *Calendar . . . Introduction*, op cit, p.48.

14. See above, p.54.

15. They are discussed in Adlington, Hugh. 'Restoration, Religion, and Law: Assize Sermons, 1660–1685', in *The Oxford Handbook of the Early Modern Sermon.* (Oxford University Press, 2011), pp.423–41.

16. Cockburn, *English Assizes*, op cit, p.239.

17. http://anglicanhistory.org/keble/keble1.html

18. Cockburn, *Calendar . . . Introduction*, op cit, pp.31 & 101.

19. Cockburn, *English Assizes*, op cit, pp.97–8.

20. Ibid, p.122.

21. Ibid, p.109.

22. Beattie, J.M. *Crime and the Courts in England, 1660-1800.* (Clarendon Press, 1986), p.336.

23. The judgement is printed (in part) in Kenyon, J.P. *The Stuart Constitution, 1603-1688: Documents and Commentary.* (Cambridge University Press, 1966), pp.428–30.

24. Cockburn, *Calendar ... Introduction*, p.113.

25 For detailed treatments of benefit of clergy, see ibid, pp.117–21, & Beattie, op cit, pp.141–6. See also Jeaffreson, John Cordy, ed. *Middlesex County Records, Vol.1.* (Middlesex County Record Society, 1886), pp.xxxiii–xxxviii.

26. Elton, G.R. *Reform and Renewal: Thomas Cromwell and the Common Weal.* (Cambridge University Press, 1973), p.136.

27. Hay, Douglas, et al. *Albion's Fatal Tree: Crime and Society in Eighteenth Century England.* (Rev ed. Verso, 2011), p.43.

28. See above, p.62.

29. National Archives Local History Research Group. *Pardons and*

Punishments: Judges' Reports on Criminals, 1783 to 1830. HO (Home Office) 47. (2 vols. List & Index Society 304-5, 2004–5).

30. For other sources, see Beattie, op cit, pp.641–3.

31. See also the Convict Transportation Registers Database www.slq.qld.gov.au/resources/family-history/convicts

32. Barnes, T.G. *Somerset 1625-1640: a County's Government during the Personal Rule.* (Harvard University Press, 1961), p.91.

33. Morrill, J.S. *The Cheshire Grand Jury, 1625-1659: a Social and Administrative Study.* (Leicester University Press, 1976), p.35.

34. Cockburn, *English Assizes*, op cit, p.180.

35. Ibid, p.xi.

36 Fowle, J.P.M., ed. *Wiltshire Quarter Sessions and Assizes, 1736.* (Wiltshire Archaeological & Natural History Society Records Branch 11, 1955), p.lxi.

37. Cockburn, *Calendar … Introduction*, pp.79–84. Knafla, Louis A., ed. *Kent at Law 1602: the County Jurisdiction: Assizes and Sessions of the Peace.* (HMSO, 1994), p.xxvi, argues that Quarter Sessions records may give more accurate information than Assize files on the residence and occupation of the accused.

38. Johnson, D.A. *Staffordshire Assize Calendars, 1842-1843.* (Collections for a History of Staffordshire 4th Series 15, 1992), pp.iv–v.

Chapter 13: Other Local Government Bodies

1. For their records, consult Stuart Raymond's series, *Vital Records for Family Historians.* 3 vols. (Family History Partnership, 2010–11). v.1. *Birth & baptism records for family historians.* v.2. *Marriage records for family historians.* v.3. *Death and burial records for family historians.*

2. Ward, W.R. 'County government since 1835', in Pugh, R.B., & Crittall, Elizabeth, eds. *A History of Wiltshire, vol.V.* (Oxford University Press, 1955), p.257.

3. Pennington, D.H., & Roots, I.A., eds. *The Committee at Stafford, 1643-1645.* (Collections for a History of Staffordshire 4th series 1, 1956), p.xxii.

4. Everitt, Alan. *The Community of Kent and the Great Rebellion, 1640-60.* (Leicester University Press, 1973), p.175.

5. Quoted by Underdown, David. *Revel, Riot and Rebellion: Popular Politics and Culture in England, 1603-1660*. (Clarendon Press, 1985), p.223.

6. Green, Mary Anne Everett, ed. *Calendar of the Committee for Compounding with Delinquents, &c., 1643-1660*. 5 vols. (HMSO, 1889–93).

7. Raymond, S.A. 'The Glamorgan Arraymen, 1642-45', *Morgannwg: the Journal of Glamorgan History* 24, 1980, pp.1–30.

8. Polden, Patrick. *A History of the County Court, 1846-1971*. (Cambridge University Press, 1999), p.51.

9. These Acts are listed in Albert, William. *The Turnpike Road System in England, 1663-1840*. (Cambridge University Press, 1972), pp.201–23.

INDEX

PLACE NAMES

PERSONAL NAMES

SUBJECT